The Open University

A221 State, Economy and Nation in Nineteenth-Century Europe

Block 3: Nation

First published in 1996 by

The Open University
Walton Hall
Milton Keynes
United Kingdom
MK7 6AA

© 1996 The Open University
Reprinted 1997, 2000 (twice)

ISBN 0 7492 1160 1

Edited, designed and typeset by The Open University.

This book is a component of the Open University course A221 *State, Economy and Nation in Nineteenth-Century Europe*. Details of this and other Open University courses are available from the Central Enquiry Service, The Open University, PO Box 200, Walton Hall, Milton Keynes, MK7 6YZ, tel.: 01908 653078.

Printed and bound in the United Kingdom by The Alden Press Ltd, Oxford.

1.4

12948C/A221block3i1.4

Contents

Acknowledgements

Grateful acknowledgement is made to the following sources for permission to reproduce material in this block:

Unit 14

Figures

Figure 1: Hoe ten-feeder news machine. (St Bride Printing Library.); *Figure 2*: James Gillray cartoon entitled *Very Slippy-Weather* and dated 10 February 1808. Copyright: British Museum; *Figure 3*: Das Einzige und Der Einige worin Deutschland einig ist. From *Facsimile Querschnitt durch den Kladderadatsch*. v.5 (Munchen, Scherz Verlag, 1965); *Figure 4*: Turning over a new leaf from the British periodical, *The Cottager and the Artisan*, for January 1866. Photo: The British Library; *Figure 5*: James Gillray cartoon, entitled *Maniac Ravings* and portraying Napoleon as 'Little Boney'. (Mansell Collection.); *Figure 6*: Cronje's surrender at Paardeberg. South African National Film, Video and Sound Archives, Pretoria; *Figure 7*: Attack on British Red Cross tent from an untitled 'fake' film. South African National Film, Video and Sound Archives, Pretoria; *Figure 8*: Set-to between John Bull and Paul Kruger. South African National Film, Video and Sound Archives, Pretoria; *Figure 9*: Religious vitality of French dioceses in 1877: estimate of religious practice by bishops and prefects. From Ralph Gibson, *A Social History of French Catholicism 1789–1914*. (London, Routledge, 1989).

Unit 11
Introduction

Prepared for the course team by Richard Bessel

Contents

Study timetable

Weeks of study	Text	Video	AC
2	Unit 11; Maps Booklet	Video 3	

Introduction

> You can joke about sex and religion, but not about nationalism.
> (Rabbi Lionel Blue, 'Thought for the Day', on 'Today', Radio 4, 11
> February 1995)

Rabbi Lionel Blue may have exaggerated a bit, but he was right to observe that nationalism is a very serious subject, one which can arouse considerable passion and about which people can be very sensitive. It is also a subject which took shape over the nineteenth century. Until the late eighteenth century, and the changes unleashed by the French Revolution, 'nation' was not the concept around which political rule was organized and legitimated nor the sentiment upon which did Europeans generally tended to base their sense of identity. Beginning a recent essay on German nationalism (and playing on the opening phrase of Nipperdey's *Deutsche Geschichte 1800–1866*, which was discussed in the course introduction), Hans-Ulrich Wehler has observed with characteristic robustness:

> In the beginning there was no nation, no nationalism, no nation-state. These all are phenomena of recent history, if their beginnings can be traced to the revolutionary upheavals of the late 18th century. For thousands of years these manifestations did not exist. If one looks at Europe, they are present neither from ancient times though the late Middle Ages nor in the old European world from the 12th to the 18th centuries. The social associations, the conceptual currents, the political institutions possess their own signature – they are not 'national', nor are they 'pre-national'. (Wehler, 1995, p.127)

Of course, this depends to some extent on where you stand. The development of the nation-state looked rather different on the Iberian peninsula, with its two long-established states, than it did in Central Europe, where Prussia-Germany was not unified until the last third of the nineteenth century. Nevertheless, it generally may be said that the nation-state, which we often take for granted as though it were the natural order of things, is something rather new – and something which largely took its shape in late eighteenth and early nineteenth-century Europe. It was during the nineteenth century that the dynastic state came largely to be superseded by the nation-state, the state which identifies with one nationality. Nineteenth-century Europe saw the growth of nationalism, both as a generalized sentiment and, increasingly, as political commitment and political programme. Even states which continued to have dynastic rulers at their head, such as the United Kingdom or Germany, increasingly came to be regarded as nation-states, whose inhabitants were united by allegedly common bounds of citizenship and nationality rather than by their bonds to a dynastic ruler. And the crumbling of multi-national empires at the end of our period – of the Austro-Hungarian and the Russian Empires during the First World War – clearly points to the declining strength of dynastic loyalty as the cement which held states together.

Nationalism, nationality, national consciousness, the nation-state: these concepts are not synonymous, but they all depend on the concept of 'nation', the third of the organizing themes of this course. Perhaps even more so than 'state' or 'economy', 'nation' is something intangible, imaginary – a concept rather than a thing. Of course, that has not prevented people from regarding a particular 'nation' very much as a thing which can be clearly delineated and defined – by citizenship, by language, by religion, by culture, by 'race'. But definitions of any particular 'nation' should not necessarily be accepted at face value. We need to question why and how people – in particular, Europeans in the nineteenth century – came to regard the 'nation' as a thing, however defined, and as something which ultimately was worth fighting and dying for. For while, as Wehler asserts, 'in the beginning' there may have been no 'nation', in the minds of millions of Europeans who marched off to war in August 1914 (at the end of the 'long nineteenth century') there certainly was.

When approaching this theme, it is important to draw the <u>distinction between nationalism as a generalized sentiment and nationalism as a source of political allegiance and political commitment.</u> The two are related but are not the same, and should not be elided with one another. It is one thing for people to feel a sense of (national) identity with one another due to shared culture or language; it is quite another for '<u>national' identity</u> to be <u>employed as a focus for a political programme and for political mobilization.</u>

The main factors which came to shape ideas of 'nation' and national consciousness in nineteenth-century Europe form the subject of the materials assembled in this block. Thus you will be working though essays and related material dealing with the following themes:

<u>Nationalism</u> (Unit 12);

<u>Language, Literacy and Education</u> (Unit 13);

<u>Culture and Religion</u> (Unit 14);

<u>State and Economy in the Creation of the Nation</u> (Unit 15).

Each of these themes forms an important aspect of the development of nationalism, national consciousness and the 'nation' in nineteenth-century Europe: for example, <u>the language</u> that one spoke and in which one was educated, <u>the religious faith</u> to which one was committed, <u>the pressures to which one was subjected by organs of the state, the economic links</u> one had to the outside world. You will examine these themes in some depth over the coming weeks. However, before you begin we believe it would be helpful to sketch out some of the terrain onto which you will be marching. That is the purpose of this Introduction. It is designed to help you to understand what is meant when we speak of 'nation' and nationalism, and to gain some idea of how different historians approach the subject and how the subject appears when approached from the vantage points of different European countries' histories during the nineteenth century. (For example, the nationalism of Poles, who did not have a state of their own in the nineteenth century, necessarily has a quite different history from that of the French, who did.)

In order to work through this Introduction you will need your cassette of Video 3 to hand (or, more accurately, in your recorder). Video 3 is similar to Video 1: It is an edited collection of interview extracts with leading historians, arranged around key subjects. In it, you will see and hear Edward Acton, John Breuilly, Norman Davies, Paul Ginsborg, Eric Hobsbawm, Wolfgang Mommsen, Paul Preston, and Robert Tombs. Following short introductory comments, first by Norman Davies and then by me, Video 3 (like Video 1) is divided into thematic sections: Nationalism, Nations, States, Education, and Habits. You may choose to view the video from beginning to end, but you need not do so if you do not wish. Here we shall take it section-by-section, beginning with the opening 'chapter' dealing with general terms with 'nationalism', what it is and where it comes from.

Video Exercise

View Video 3, Section 1, 'Nationalism', pp.61–429. This begins with a long exposition on nineteenth-century nationalism by Edward Acton (whose own research has centred on Russia), followed by observations by Eric Hobsbawm, Norman Davies, and Paul Ginsborg. While listening, consider what the four historians assembled here regard as most important for the growth of nationalism in nineteenth-century Europe.

Discussion

It is fairly obvious that the four historians speaking here approach nationalism from various angles. However, there are some basic points of agreement. The first is the importance of ideas. To start with Edward Acton, whose lengthy comment begins this section: Acton views nationalism as support for ideas, movements, and sees its most important carriers as the educated urban élites. There is also agreement that the French revolution was crucial to the development of modern nationalism in nineteenth-century Europe. As Acton notes, with the French Revolution came the principle that the people have the right to rule themselves (as opposed to the idea of Divine Right of kings or the supranational reach of the Church) – a principle which gained increasing support in the course of the nineteenth century; and with popular, national self-determination came the possibility of a redistribution of power within society. A further important point raised by Acton concerns the changing political location of nationalism in nineteenth-century Europe, from left to right, which constituted one of the most important political shifts of the century.

Eric Hobsbawm also begins with the idea that the people have the right to rule themselves, when he speaks of nationalism as a by-product of democratization, of the involvement of 'the people' as a political actor. The question which follows is, of course: 'Who then are "the people"?' This is something which Hobsbawm addresses when he points out that, initially (by which he means with the French Revolution), 'nation' was a political concept: that the 'nation' was essentially state-defined, a people linked by political bonds. However, according to Hobsbawm in the course of the nineteenth century the idea of the people as members of communities (rather than polities) came to define the 'nation'; as Hobsbawm points out, the novelty of the new nationalism of the nineteenth century is that it assumed that being part of a national community is the prerequisite for being part of the political community.

Paul Ginsborg too underscores the importance of the French Revolution, and he points to the two basic views of nationalism in nineteenth-century Europe: The first is the democratic nationalism of the French and American revolutions, linked to liberation and revolution from below, and undermined by the failure of the revolutions of 1848. The second is the liberal nationalism linked to capitalist development and control from above (and thus linked to dynastic regimes), the nationalism of Bismarck and Cavour. It was this second form of nationalism which, as Ginsborg points out, ultimately was successful in Europe. This, it may seem, paralleled the political shift of nationalism in nineteenth-century Europe which Acton outlined.

Finally, Norman Davies, whose main research area has been Poland, approaches the subject from a rather different perspective, focusing on two contrasting rival promoters of nationalism: governments/states, setting out to create a homogeneity and a state-based nationalism; and movements, setting out to create a grass-roots nationalism *against* a dominant nationalism (e.g. of nationalist movements in Ireland and Poland). Here it is worth thinking about how the nationalisms which Davies describes differ from the broad picture painted at the outset by Acton. Davies's account makes it appear that nationalism is something which either is promoted by governments or which develops from the bottom up, from popular movements. This is rather different from what is said by Acton, who sees nationalism as based on national consciousness which in turn largely is the work of educated, urban élites. This may provide a good example of how different national focus (Poland or Ireland as opposed to France or Russia) might lead a historian towards different sorts of conclusions.

Video Exercise

View Video 3, Section 2, 'Nations', pp.430–729. The subject of this section is how various European nations have come into being and have defined themselves. In this Section, you will hear Robert Tombs discussing France, Wolfgang Mommsen discussing Germany, Paul Ginsborg discussing Italy, Edward Acton discussing Russia, and Norman Davies discussing eastern European Jews. Each discusses the 'nation' in question in different terms. What, outlined in the interview extracts compiled here, appear to be the defining characteristics of each 'nation' considered, and how do they differ from one another?

Discussion

Let us go through this one by one.

Tombs, discussing France, asserts that for the French the 'nation' is not some static, given entity but rather something always thought of as being created. There are two quite different views of this: the revolutionary view, whereby the French turn themselves into a nation in 1789; and the traditional, conservative view of the French nation being created by its monarchs. Either way, the French 'nation' is something made, as a deliberate act. In either case, however, there is relatively little question about what constitutes 'France', which constituted a clearly defined territory and was governed by a strongly centralized state.

In the case of Germany, discussed by Wolfgang Mommsen, the problem was how, once modern national movement destroyed the old political system, to create a nation in an area inhabited by many nationalities. There the state – specifically the 'small-German' state of the German Empire established in 1871 (i.e. 'small' in that it excluded Austria) – eventually came to define the German 'nation', as Germans began to identify with the German Empire and not concern themselves too greatly about Germans who lived outside (say, in today's Austria, Bohemia, Moravia, the South Tyrol).

The Italian case, discussed by Paul Ginsborg, offers an interesting contrast with that of Germany, as it is debatable whether one meaningfully can speak of an Italian 'nation' in the nineteenth century at all. This contrast is remarkable, as both Germany and Italy were 'latecomers', in that

trajectory =
(planeetat, annutsu)
rata

they were unified only in the second half of the nineteenth century. It is worth thinking, therefore, about why their subsequent historical trajectories differed from one another – for example, whether this was a function of Prussia-Germany's more rapid industrial development or the different practice of her state bureaucracy (themes which you have examined in the first two blocks). Ginsborg notes that at the time of Italian unification 'Italy' was no more than a geographical entity; indeed, some have argued that 'Italy' did not become a 'nation' until well into the twentieth century! There the great mass of the population was not involved in, but excluded from the benefits of nation-building; they were, in the oft-repeated phrase of Antonio Gramsci, 'passive' spectators in the creation of the 'nation'. As a consequence of this 'passive revolution', instead of 'vertical' (i.e. national) solidarities, 'horizontal' (class) solidarities were particularly strong in Italy.

The terms with which Edward Acton approaches the question of how the Russian 'nation' is defined are quite different. The point he stresses here is perhaps an obvious one: the importance of the vastness of the Russian Empire. From this he posits the relative unimportance of national identity in the Russian case – 'unless you lived on the borderlands'. (Further along in the Video, in the section on 'Habits', Acton also stresses the importance of the Russian Orthodox Church in defining the Russian 'nation'.) This should prompt you to think about what factors may provoke a sense of national identity (e.g. contact and conflict with other 'nations') and what do not.

Finally, Norman Davies discusses a subject which, at first sight, might appear fundamentally different from the nationalism discussed hitherto: Jewish nationalism, Zionism. But how different was it? As Davies describes it, Jewish nationalism appears to have followed an almost classic development of European nationalisms as Jews began to view themselves as not simply a religious community. Parallel to the aspirations of other groups without a state of their own – for example, the Poles, the Ukrainians – Jews who turned to Zionism had political aspirations for the control over their own political destiny as a 'nation'. What set it apart from other radical nationalist movements in late nineteenth-century Europe was that the national homeland to which Zionists aspired was not on the European continent. Of course it needs to be remembered that a Jewish homeland in Palestine was a minority aspiration among European Jews in the nineteenth century, both in the relatively assimilated Jewish communities of western Europe and in the more traditionally religious communities of eastern Europe, and that support for Zionism was in large measure a reaction to the pogroms and persecution prevalent in the Russian Empire. But it is worth thinking about how this perhaps unlikely nationalism was influenced by general currents in Europe at the time.

So, what conclusions can we draw from these discussions? When one proceeds from the general topic of 'nationalism' to a consideration of 'nations', the different national historiographies start asserting themselves. Are the different emphases due to the fact that national histories are unique, or rather to the fact that historians are considering different issues in the different cases? I suggest that it is a combination of the two. Video 3, Section 2 provides a good example of how national historiographies shape the ways in which general themes are conceived; this is worth remembering as you work your way through the units in the block, and consider general themes in the light of particular national cases and vice versa.

Video Exercise

View Video 3, Section 3, 'States', pp.730–992. Clearly states played a crucial role in both defining and promoting nationality. This is something about which all the historians interviewed for this video could agree. The question I want you to consider now is: What was that role? How do the historians, whose comments are excerpted in this section, view that role? (You will find it useful to look at Map 4 in the Maps Booklet (which shows the ethnic diversity of the Austro-Hungarian empire), with reference to at least part of what Eric Hobsbawm and John Breuilly in particular have to say.)

Discussion

Here it is best to begin with John Breuilly, whose comments open this section and who asserts that: 'The modern state in effect creates the kind of society to which the nationalist ideal appears to correspond'. (Later on he states: 'I would argue that the *modern* state tends to produce nationality'.) He notes that central to the modern state are the ideas of citizenship (and citizenship rights) and territoriality – which creates the need to define who has these citizenship rights within a given territory (i.e. who is a member of the 'nation'). He also notes that the modern state of the nineteenth century created new ways in which political power is contested (e.g. elections) on a national basis.

Eric Hobsbawm poses the interesting question of whether a dynastic nationalism should have been a viable alternative, and suggests that 'theoretically' there is no reason why this should not have been successful in Austria or Russia as it was in the United Kingdom. Is this wishful thinking? John Breuilly gives a good reason why it should not have been similarly successful, drawing on the example of the Habsburg state of the Austro-Hungarian Empire – a multi-national empire which finally was undone by national conflict, and where ethnic complexity will be apparent from Map 4 (in the Maps Booklet). According to Breuilly, because of the fact that the Habsburg Empire was a modernizing state (industrializing, educating, etc.) and that 'the modern state tends to produce nationality', in effect the Habsburg state helped generate the tensions which, as it headed for defeat in the First World War, were to destroy it.

Norman Davies has a different focus, as he is concerned with a 'nation' which developed in *opposition* to states: the Polish nation. Here the role of the state, in this instance the Prussian-German state, was to provoke a sense of national identity among the Poles in eastern Prussia by trying to suppress it.

Paul Preston, examining Spain, offers yet another angle on the role of the state in creating the 'nation'. The state which Preston describes is perhaps not the 'modern state' to which Breuilly attaches such importance, but it certainly was a strong centralizing state. This gave rise to the apparent paradox that in Spain modernity was on the periphery, reacting against the central state. And whereas modern economic interests in Spain were not a force for national unity, the Spanish army was – in Preston's words, 'the nearest thing to an instrument of the modern state'.

It should also be noted that when examining the role of the state in 'nation' formation, it is necessary to distinguish the various processes and the different roles of the state, and not just lump them all together. When commenting on one of the A221 units while still in draft, John Breuilly (in his role as course assessor) observed: 'One should distinguish between how the *modern* state promotes nationality through such processes as legal unification and intervention and how the *nation* state promotes nationality through such processes as discrimination in favour of one nationality'. This is a distinction which you should keep in mind as you work through this block.

Video Exercise

View Video 3, Section 4, 'Language and Education', pp.993–1169. There are two general aspects to this theme: on the one hand (following on from the theme of Section 3), the interventions and role of the state (which operates schools, imposes language requirements, discriminates in favour of or against the speakers of certain languages); on the other, language as defining national culture and thus nationality. In this section, Robert Tombs, Norman Davies and Edward Acton speak. Which of these two general aspects of the subject do they address?

Discussion

Tombs's theme here is not education (although education was extremely centralized in France), but language – the question of whether people spoke French and what the significance of this may have been. As Tombs points out (and was pointed out some time ago by Eugene Weber in his justly famous *Peasants into Frenchmen*), until the 1870s most people in France did not speak French as their first language, and someone travelling from Paris into the provinces often would find it difficult to be understood. France, that centralized model of the nation-state, was a multicultural society for most of the nineteenth century. But does this mean that the French were not a 'nation'? Tombs thinks not. (And, if you think back to Eric Hobsbawm's discussion of the 'nation' as a political community, you may see that there are good grounds to accept this interpretation, especially with regard to France.) But *why* does language in the French case appear not to have been connected to patriotism? Thinking back to a point which Edward Acton made in Section 1, perhaps this has to do with the importance of educated élites as the developers and carriers of national consciousness, of the restricted nature of the 'political nation'. The question of whether or not the great mass of people in the provinces spoke French therefore might not have been of major importance in giving them a sense of French nationality.

Norman Davies and Edward Acton discuss the other aspect: education and the interventions of the state. Davies notes, for example, how the Prussian army was used as an instrument of homogenization, spreading literacy in the *German* language among Polish men who were drafted, and how during the 1880s and 1890s the Russian authorities attempted to spread the Russian language among the Polish population of the Empire. Acton stresses the close correlation between the spread of education and nationalism; particularly in a multi-national empire. As he notes, when the educational system is extended the question necessarily arises: In what language do you educate? As the comments of Norman Davies indicate, the answers to this question often provoked nationalist sentiment. Note as well that here (in the Russian Empire, including Congress Poland) the people being educated, in Polish or Russian, were almost by definition the élite; throughout the nineteenth century the majority of the population of the Russian Empire was illiterate.

Video Exercise

View Video 3, Section 5, 'Habits', pp.1169–1438. This section of the video opens with an critique by John Breuilly of the idea that there is any necessarily inherent essential quality which distinguishes a particular national group (i.e. his debunking the idea of 'Germanness' or 'Frenchness'). Instead, he suggests that 'habits' offers a better descriptive tool with which to discuss nationality. But what 'habits', and where do these habits come from?

Discussion

Breuilly himself offers some incisive answers to this question. For him, the interventions of the state are crucially important: He notes that it may well be that if there are national institutions (such as schools with national curricula), then consequently there may develop 'national' habits. However, Breuilly remains sceptical about the import of these habits as an indicator of 'national' identity. Tombs appears to take a different view: he highlights one very important 'habit' of the French – having far fewer children than did other Europeans in the nineteenth century – and suggests that this was one thing which made people from different localities and different walks of life 'French'. But in explaining this French 'habit', Tombs focuses on the institutions and social experiences which make this reasonable behaviour, which in a way buttresses Breuilly's point.

In Russia, in the view of Edward Acton, Orthodoxy played a key role, as did identification with the land and simple honest values (as opposed to the cosmopolitan, urban, capitalist values which allegedly characterized other, western nationalities). And, in conclusion, Paul Preston notes both the enormous disparities between different groups of Spaniards and the literary origins of our picture of the habits which are taken to constitute Spanish culture and nationality – a point which neatly links back to the opening point about the importance of educated urban élites as promoters of national consciousness.

Conclusion

Obviously, this short introduction gives only an overview of Video 3. But it also points ahead. Its purpose has been to familiarize you with the main themes which will arise in the materials which follow, materials which will allow you to examine these and related subjects in considerably more detail and with considerably greater analytical rigour. This introduction thus is designed to offer you something of an agenda of questions, and a catalogue of ideas and perspectives with which to approach the materials in this block. When working your way through this block, and when approaching the TMA questions, try to apply critically the perspectives presented here.

One final point: It should be fairly obvious by now that the theme of this block is closely related to the themes of the previous two blocks. As the comments of the historians assembled on Video 3 make abundantly clear, the development of the 'nation', of nationalism and national consciousness in nineteenth-century Europe, was inseparable from the development of the state and of the economy. So, when working your way through this part of the course, try to draw upon what you already have learned.

References

Wehler, H-U. (1995), 'Welche Probleme kann ein deutscher Nationalismus lösen?', in Hans-Ulrich Wehler, *Die Gegenwart als Geschichte. Essays*, C.H. Beck, Munich.

Unit 12
Nationalism

Prepared for the course team by Bill Purdue

Contents

Study timetable

Weeks of Study	Text	Video	AC
2	Unit 12; Anderson		

Objectives

By the end of this unit you should:

1   be familiar with some theories and debates about nationalism;

2   have an understanding of the varieties of European nationalisms in the nineteenth century and the time scales of their development;

3   be able to consider some specific examples of the development of nationalism and nation-states.

The nature of nationalism

> Nationalism is a doctrine invented in Europe at the beginning of the nineteenth century ... Briefly, the doctrine holds that humanity is naturally divided into nations, that nations are known by certain characteristics which can be ascertained, and that the only legitimate type of government is national self-government. (Kedourie, 1967, p.9)

Just as there have always been rulers and ruled and dominant and subordinate groups, so there have always been those who have been, or have seen themselves as being oppressed, while the need for rulers or churches to maintain control over territories or populations has always demanded some focus for unity or discipline. But the view that the nation is the obvious political unit and nationality its cement, with the corollary that national minorities within a state are thwarted in self-realization, is distinctly modern. What is more debatable is whether the dynamics of nationalism are themselves modern.

Elie Kedourie's statement above may seem startling. We are not used to thinking of nationalism as a doctrine or an ideology in the same way as we think of socialism or liberalism for we consider it to be natural, basic or atavistic rather than a doctrine. To say that it was 'invented' runs in the face of such assumptions while to locate the 'invention' in a particular era seems akin to believing that, on or about a certain date, human nature changed. Yet, we must remind ourselves of two things: that what Kedourie is talking about is not 'patriotism', nor that innate tendency to identify with our own kind and our own place, both of which certainly existed before 1800; and that the doctrine to which he refers has proved so pervasive that we tend to accept national self-determination as almost axiomatically a good thing.

A further complication is that the development of nationalism in the nineteenth century was paralleled by the development of the academic discipline of history. One could indeed argue that the spirit of nationalism, not only imbued much historical writing, but was a central reason for the growth of interest in history. When historians viewed the past they tended to do so with the 'common sense' of nationalism in their minds which enabled them to arrange past developments into scenarios of the emergence of nations, by which peoples were always struggling towards self-determination, and to argue that nations existed well before the nineteenth century.

What we can call the modernist approach to nationalism is argued by many historians and social scientists other than Kedourie. Ernest Gellner (1983), E.J. Hobsbawm (1990), Benedict Anderson (1991) and John Breuilly (1982) all see nationalism as a modern innovation. Although there are many disagreements between them as to the specific causes of the phenomenon, they concur in placing its birth in the context of industrialization, democratic ideology and rationalism. Kedourie attributes considerable influence to philosophers and to the Romantic movement. He sees the decline in religious belief and the rise of a more secular society as having left a vacuum. As traditional values were eroded politics replaced religion. Immanuel Kant (1724–1804) viewed man as autonomous and made the individual a free and independent being in pursuit of perfection. This idea of the self-determination of the individual was somewhat perversely developed by Johann Gottlieb Fichte (1762–1814) who considered that true individual self-realization could only be achieved when the individual identified himself with a greater whole. The state was higher than the individual and, rather than the state being there to serve the individual, the individual was there to serve it. Kedourie sees this doctrine in conjunction with the ideas of Johann Gottfreid Herder (1744–1803) on the significance of language differences as fundamental in creating nationalism. Although Kedourie gives pre-eminence to the German philosophic tradition, he also acknowledges the influence of Jean-Jacques Rousseau (1712–88), who argued that it was necessary for the moral unity of social life that men had a common aim; they must exchange their selfish individual aims for a general will and a 'civic religion'. But it is not just the philosophic messengers that Kedourie sees as crucial for what was also essential was the existence of an educated class, excluded from power who were receptive to the message. The key group in the promotion of nationalism was the professional middle class.

Gellner (1983) sees nationalism as arising from the need of modern societies for cultural homogeneity. Pre-industrial societies can tolerate a high degree of diversity including ethnic and linguistic diversity. They are stratified and communities are local. Such societies have a High Culture and Low Cultures, the former being the cosmopolitan culture of the élite, medieval Latin learning or the art, manners and mores of the courts, and the latter the highly localized culture of the peasantry. By contrast modern societies are egalitarian, mobile and homogeneous. Nationality is produced by the transition to industrialization and nations are defined by a language which is the basis of an educational system. A rudimentary version of the High Culture is given national form, is closely linked with a standardized national language and the new national culture merges with political identity.

Hobsbawm (1983) argues that the concept of the nation was associated with the 'invention of tradition', a process encouraged by élites in order to legitimize their power amidst economic change and the rise of democratic ideas. States and their ruling classes could find in national feeling a means of securing loyalty to replace or supplement those traditional bonds such as loyalty to a ruler or religion.

Benedict Anderson (1991) sees the nation as an imagined political community made possible by the rise of new means of communication, primarily printing. The newspaper and the novel enabled communities to be psychologically enlarged while journalists and novelists acted as the carriers of national ideas.

John Breuilly (1982) has identified the rise of the bureaucratic state as the formative development. Nationalism resolved tensions between the state and civil society by giving the state a primacy based upon historic and cultural legitimacy as a historic community. By eliding the distinctions between the concepts of the nation as a cultural community and the nation as a political community a pseudo solution was provided to the problem of the relationship between the state and society.

Exercise   What do you think these explanations have in common?

Discussion You would do well to say that they are all based upon the idea of a fundamental change, a watershed, in the nature of European society. Although such change is located in the late eighteenth and the nineteenth centuries, an explanation like Benedict Anderson's posits such change as the maturation of a relatively long-term development, the coming of printing in the fourteenth century. Explanations like Gellner's and Hobsbawm's with their emphasis upon industrial capitalism and democracy see cause and effect within a shorter time span as does Kedourie's more philosopher-oriented argument. All point to the weakening of more traditional sources of political and social authority and the role of nationalism in filling this vacuum. All see nineteenth-century nationalism as a new phenomenon and to some degree an artificial one, though Hobsbawm goes furthest in this respect in that he sees nationalisms as almost deliberately 'invented'.

You will not be surprised to learn, for you know by now that historians are an argumentative lot, that this modernist view does not go unchallenged. It is true that few historians would now see nationalism as 'primordial' (existing at or from the beginning) in the way that some nineteenth-century authors, who were at the once historians and founding fathers of national movements, did (writers like Frantisec Palacky and Eoin MacNeill saw, respectively, the Czechs and the Irish as always nations struggling for independence through time). A school of contemporary thinking on nationalism does, however, take what is known as the *ethnicist* approach, arguing that, though modern nationalism and the nation-state have a modern form, particularly in the emphasis placed upon citizenship, the modern nation built upon ethno-cultural identities that had a long history. Anthony Smith (1986), perhaps the leading ethnicist, considers that modern nationalism was shaped by previous ethnic identities which were shaped over time by such factors as the settlement of formerly migratory peoples and by wars with neighbours. He discerns two types of pre-modern national feeling: that which is felt exclusively or predominantly by ruling groups and develops around a centralized state before spreading from the top down to form a nation-state; and a popular ethnic identity, usually found where the ruling groups are culturally and often linguistically distinct from those they rule. In the first group come those nations which first formed nation-states, England, France and Spain, while in the second come the nationalisms of 'subject peoples', the various forms of Slav nationalism for instance.

Exercise I would like you to read Anderson, pp. 204–6, and then answer the following questions.

1   Does Anderson see nationalism as a modern development?

2   What event or development does he see as marking the birth of modern nationalism?

3   What sections of society does he see as particularly influential in helping to promote national feeling?

4   How significant does he consider nationalism to be?

Specimen Answers

1 He sees it as growing in influence from the late eighteenth century but he doesn't actually say that it's a new phenomenon. He acknowledges that modern nationalism is built upon age-old instincts such as patriotism and dislike of foreigners, and detects 'an embryonic consciousness of some distinct collective personality' as early as the times of Edward the Confessor or Charlemagne. Anderson is thus a bit ambivalent on the question as to whether nationalism in the nineteenth century was a totally new phenomenon, though he is clear that it had a new dynamism and took new forms.

2 He attributes enormous importance to the French Revolution: 'The years 1789–91 thus saw a quite unprecedented assertion of belief in the nation as an ultimate value before which others must give way. Modern nationalism, intolerant, demanding and creative, the nationalism of the masses, had been born.'

3 What he calls middle-class groups, which were growing in numbers and importance and helped national consciousness evolve.

4 He considers that it is enormously important: 'The most important political fact of the nineteenth century in Europe was the growth of nationalism'.

The big question we have identified so far is the degree to which nineteenth-century nationalism was a new phenomenon with its birth in the context of the French Revolution. Our starting point as ever must be the immediate past. Anderson, you will have noted, attaches supreme importance to the emergence in the early modern period of powerful monarchies – France, Spain, England, Russia and Sweden – which, he argues created much of the political and territorial framework within which nineteenth-century nationalism was to function. What these monarchies had in common was not merely that they were powerful, an attribute that they shared with Austria, the Ottoman Empire and Prussia, but that they had some claim to be considered nation-states. However, Russia, ironically, was at the point of becoming less so, as the expansion of its frontiers diluted its Russian character by adding to its already considerable ethnic diversity. But how important was this characteristic compared to the facts that all were monarchies and all had established religions? In so far as their populations had national identities and patriotisms, had these much in common with nineteenth-century nationalism?

France, as Kedourie has written, 'is not a state because the French constitute a nation, but [it is] rather that the French state is the outcome of dynastic ambitions, of circumstances, of lucky wars, of administrative and diplomatic skills' (Kedourie, 1967, p.78). Late eighteenth-century Britain, we may remind ourselves, would have been a rather different state if late medieval English kings had succeeded in hanging on to their French possessions, always a greater priority for them than their designs on Scotland. Eighteenth-century Europe was a society of states not of nations. Geography, warfare and dynastic marriages had resulted in a number of major states such as England, France, and Spain, that were relatively homogeneous in language and culture and whose peoples had a sense of shared history. Their geographic cohesiveness and relative national homogeneity gave them certain advantages over states which were composed of disparate territories and varied ethnic and language groups, but it would be rash to conclude that it was their national characters that gave them their legitimacy and reason for being. Allegiance to monarchs and faith in common religions were difficult to disentangle from patriotism while there is little evidence that language, ethnicity and culture were seen as the obvious basis for political units.

It is indeed possible to deny that modern nationalism was conceivable within the old monarchical context. Clark (1994) has written that, while the monarchical tie remained in place:

> ... unchallenged except by denominational or dynastic rivalry, it was almost impossible for a different sense of identity to arise: it had no theoretical framework into which to flow. By contrast, cultural stereotypes were familiar, lovingly tended and satirically exploited in the old society; but they existed for decades even centuries, without generating 'nationalism'. It was the permanent disruption of a monarchical tie, in America in 1776–83 and France in 1789–93, which compelled the development of an alternative framework of self identity, built slowly, with difficulty and immense effort around the presumed coherence of those with a common language (ignoring their profound divisions of dialect, vocabulary and accent), a common culture (ignoring even larger regional variations) or shared ethnicity (however hard this was to demonstrate empirically). (Clark, 1994, pp.52–3)

Eighteenth-century European society was for the upper orders a cosmopolitan world and for the common people, the vast majority of the population, a local world. Orders or ranks might correspond to ethnicity but to be an aristocrat or a peasant was infinitely more important than that peasants might be Slav and aristocrats German or Magyar, though no doubt things worked better when both shared more or less the same language. It is dubious whether many peasants conceived of themselves as belonging to ethnic groups, never mind national groups, and immigrants to the USA from east and central Europe generally described themselves as from a locality rather than as Albanians, Slovaks or Estonians. As Hobsbawm (1990) points out, the word Estonian only came into use in the 1860s and before that the peasantry had simply called themselves 'maarahvas' or country people. Royalty at the top really had no nationality for they had after all to be prepared to change it when they married or inherited. (George III was very unusual when he rejoiced in the name of Briton and Queen Victoria was more conventional a century and more later when she objected to the future George V joining the Royal Navy on the grounds that it would make him too British.) The cosmopolitanism of the aristocracies can be seen in the readiness of so confident an aristocracy as the British to accept that culture and polish were to be acquired abroad on the Grand Tour, and in the almost universal acceptance that French was the language of courts and of diplomats. In much of Europe peasant communities lived only dimly aware of the wider entities, states, to which they were supposed to belong and, if they occasionally revolted against those who taxed them, they did so in the name of traditional local rights, not because those who taxed them spoke a different language. There were exceptions to this: in

Britain with its more liberal and individualistic social and economic order, the population seems to have been comparatively mobile with a surprising proportion having lived at some time in London, while in general the extremes of localism seem to have been in eastern and central rather than in western and northern Europe. We can see however the force of Anderson's argument that it was the growth of the middle stratas of society that was likely to foster a national rather than a cosmopolitan or local outlook. Overall, however, association for the majority was local rather than national.

The rationalism of the Enlightenment was the intellectual cutting edge that weakened the bonds of allegiance to monarchies and of religious certainties. It aimed to free men and women and enable them to choose their forms of civic association. No less than what it opposed, it was an inherently cosmopolitan mindset which contained the seeds of its own demise in that having destroyed the traditional allegiances, it found them replaced by one no more rational but more exclusive, nationalism. Allegiance to a monarch was after all inclusive, an alien was not of a different nationality but one who owed allegiance to a different king and all who came to live within a state could swear allegiance to the monarch of that state. Ethnic nationalism was to be exclusive.

The growth of nationalism took place over different time scales in different parts of Europe, and took varied forms depending on such factors as whether or not existing states conformed roughly to ethnic divides, or contained many ethnic and linguistic groups, the social structures and degree of economic development of states and the strength of religion.

Exercise   I would now like you to return to Anderson's section, 'The Triumph of Nationalism', pp.204–24, and answer the following questions.

1   To what extent did the French Revolutionary and Napoleonic periods see a rise in national feeling in Europe?

2   What headway had nationalism made by 1815?

3   What factors made for the further development of nationalism in the nineteenth century?

Specimen Answers   1   The victories of the French revolution and the Napoleonic Empire did much to stimulate national feeling. The expansion of French power both led to emulation of its national ethos and to opposition in the form of a hostile reaction which stimulated other and often conservative national feelings. National resistance to Napoleon in Russia and Spain was much imbued with religious feeling in contrast to the essentially secular nationalism of Revolutionary and Napoleonic France. Such conservative national feeling could have a monarchical element.

2   Nationalism in 1815 was weak although it was a force and a growing one. In Germany the great majority of the population was scarcely touched by it and the aspirations of its proponents were limited. In Italy the peasantry were scarcely conscious of being Italian and identification with localities and existing states was strong, while Italian was hardly a national language such were its regional variations.

3 ‖ The influence of philosophers, historians, poets and political thinkers: von Humboldt, von Ranke, Herder, Fichte, Hegel and Schlier-
macher in Germany; Mazzini in Italy; Michelet and Comte in France;
Palacky in Bohemia: and Koskinen in Finland. All in different ways
could be seen as encouraging the idea of the nation, its unique identity and its mission.

Along with the writing of national histories went a growing interest in folklore and folk culture. All over Europe the songs, dances, customs and traditional dress of the peasantry were lovingly researched (and sometimes
invented). Nineteenth-century nationalism, Anderson argues was above all
'linguistic nationalism'. Along with this came the growth of mass literacy
and books and newspapers making possible wider identities. For dominant
languages the printed word, like state education, was a means of unifying
and integrating, but for nationalities who were beginning to perceive themselves as subjugated it could be a statement of separatism.

Anderson also mentions the influence of racialism on nationalism
from the mid-nineteenth century, making it more difficult for national feeling to be about the voluntary association of different peoples in a state
because of shared values, and much more a matter of birth.

Any broad chronology or pattern in the development of nationalism
in the period is undermined by the different time scales at which its manifestations occurred in different parts of Europe and by its regional variety.

If nationalism sprang from the pens of philosophers and the reception of their ideas by the educated but career-less, as Kedourie would have
it, how did it establish a popular base? As Gellner (1994) has put it: 'It is
well established history that no bombs have been thrown on behalf of
Kant's doctrine of the priority status of categories'. Yet if Gellner is right
and socio-economic change is all important, why did nationalism flourish
in some of the least industrialized areas of Europe and why were small
intelligentsias in largely agrarian societies so influential as promoters of
nationalism?

A paradox in the development of nineteenth-century nationalism is
the romantic importance attached to the peasantry as the true custodians
of the national spirit by those furthest removed from them, those fuglemen
of national revival, the dissident intellectuals. As John Breuilly (1982,
p.340) has tellingly observed of the Czech intellectual and nationalist
Palacky, who thought he had found the 'natural' Czech nation in 'the people': 'The Czechs Palacky studied did not and could not have produced
Palacky himself or the complex and changing society of Bohemia which
gave rise to Czech nationalism'. Much the same could be said of those
graduates of Trinity College, Dublin, who, in the late nineteenth century
used their anglicized minds to discern the sterling virtues of a peasant way
of life, that the peasantry itself was only too eager to leave. Nationalism
was both influenced by and encouraged the growth of antiquarianism and
the study of folk traditions, music and dances, which came to be seen as
the repositories of the national culture submerged by cosmopolitanism or
foreign rule and threatened by the standardization of socio-economic
change. Contradictions abounded: no-one is more psychologically removed

from a particular peasant culture than the expert on peasant cultures; peasant languages and patois had to be standardized before they could form national languages; and nationalists have both drawn on tradition and when in power sought to make their national state more formidable economically and militarily and thus more modern.

The view that 'modernization', especially the decay of religious belief and the rise of secular attitudes, propelled nationalism has to contend with the awkward fact that a number of nationalisms, Polish and Irish nationalism for instance, have fed off religious feeling or that a central distinction between Serbs and Croats is religion.

Historians have tended, however, like Anderson (p.224) to distinguish between the consolidating and on the whole liberal nationalism of states in northern Europe which had existed before the evolution of modern nations, the unifying nationalism of Germany and Italy, and the divisive nationalism of east-central and south-eastern Europe. We can also distinguish, however, not just a west–east drift but a left–right drift, in that nationalism in the early nineteenth century tended to be liberal and secular, and much late nineteenth-century nationalism tended to be xenophobic and sectarian as a nationalism that was at least in theory 'civic', gave way to ethnic nationalism. We must therefore look out for changes in the character of nationalism not only between countries but within them.

We will now consider examples of the development of national feeling across this spectrum.

France

As we have seen France is seen by historians as the key state in the history of nationalism. The French Revolution, it is held, overthrew loyalty to dynasty and replaced it with the idea of national sovereignty to be exercised by self-governing citizens and thus opened the way to the triumph of the principle of nationalism. As one authority has put it:

> With this transformation came a new iconography and set of rituals. The emblems of monarchial rule sanctified by religious rites and arcane aristocratic codes were replaced by a national flag (the tricolour), a stirring national anthem (the Marseillaise) and great open-air festivals of public dedication (oath taking) to the commemoration of the nation, which were marked by mass participation. A new political religion was being formed in which the people, now deified, worshipped themselves. (Hutchinson, 1994, p.39)

The revolution and the wars that followed it were, notoriously, to have a radical influence on the rest of Europe through the transmission of revolutionary ideas, not least the claim that the nation was the sole source of political power, the disappearance of old states like Venice and Genoa, the end of the Holy Roman Empire, the expansion of France's frontiers and the emergence of new nationalisms, in part a French export, in part a reaction to French hegemony. Appropriately enough the word 'nationalism' first appears in 1798–9 in the writings of the Jesuit Abbé Barruel; he used it to mean scorn and hatred towards foreigners.

But what of its long-term influence on France itself? France, despite the efforts of the armies of the Republic and the Empire, was no larger in 1815 than she had been under the old regime but even under the restored Bourbons, she was much more a nation-state.

The initial rationalist, secular and democratic thrust of the revolution did not necessarily point in the direction of nationalism for there was an ambivalence as to whether the source of authority should be simply the voluntary association of persons, who were thus a people, which equalled a nation or whether the people or the nation was pre-determined by existing common characteristics. The Declaration of Rights of Man and Citizen of 1791 proclaimed that, 'the source of all authority resides essentially in the nation; no group, no individual may exercise authority not emanating expressly therefrom'. The Declaration of Rights of 1795 stated that: 'Each people is independent and sovereign, whatever the number of people who compose it and the extent of the territory it occupies. This sovereignty is inalienable'. But what constituted a people and what a nation? The emphasis was upon popular will and upon 'the people' as opposed to monarch or aristocracy. There was no proviso that 'the people' would correspond to a language, a common culture, a common historic past or ethnic grouping. Yet, if the Revolution can be seen as initially almost international, French governments were soon proclaiming the necessity for all Frenchmen to speak French, and the emphasis upon one sovereign power, the national legislature, led to a much more centralized and uniform state than the so-called absolute monarchs had ever hoped for. The state included Alsatians, Basques, Bretons, Catalans and Corsicans, but it was a French state and the tendency was for state power to be utilized to make its inhabitants more French. Anderson mentions the suggestion that no French citizen be allowed to marry unless he could speak, read and write in French. If it had previously been as, or more, important to be an aristocrat, a Breton or Gascon than French, the impact of the revolutionary principle of national sovereignty was to remove the local laws, special jurisdictions and traditional privileges which had divided Frenchmen in the past. It soon became clear that the people was the nation, and that the state both represented the will of the nation and had the duty of making the nation more perfect because more uniform. France under the Republic and the Empire saw a considerable extension of state power which continued the momentum towards centralization and the eradication of differences between different parts of France and different kinds of French men and women. The state was to a degree forging the nation. Napoleon's Civil Code of 1804 was the clearest demonstration of the extension of state power and, while he re-established the Catholic Church with the concordat with Rome of 1801, the Church was in effect subject to the state.

The nineteenth-century state was to increase its effectiveness and its control over the population via a number of instruments among them cadres of loyal officials, the army and a state educational system. The very expansion of these instruments provided enthusiastic supporters of the state by providing employment for those middle social groups which historians have considered the cement of the national state. Not only did Napoleon encourage a landowning upper class, which included both nobles and rich commoners, but he sought to establish a professional state

bureaucracy, salaried and to some degree meritocratic, and a state education system whose secondary schools, although only for the well-to-do,
were part of a highly centralized system. The rationalized and centralized
administration of the Napoleonic Empire with its *conseil d'état* and the
prefects was to continue substantially unchanged until the Third Republic.

The efforts of the restored monarchy to re-establish the rituals and
mystique of the monarchy were largely unsuccessful as Anderson (p.64)
demonstrates but it would be wrong to conclude that France after 1815 was
securely cohesive and confident in a new secular identity as the French
people. Few historians would view the revolutionary and Napoleonic periods as marking a clean break with the past and would emphasize the deep
divisions in French society consequent upon the Revolution. National feeling could only replace loyalty to monarch and religion as the focus of identity if there was agreement on the nation and its past. Anderson argues that
the monarchy was absolutely necessary to France after 1815 for a constitutional monarchy was what divided Frenchmen least. The Orleanist Monarchy 1830–48, with its King of the French rather than a King of France,
can be seen as an attempt to reconcile the monarchical tradition with the
national ethos. The great problem for France as a nation-state was that the
recent past was contested rather than shared, a problem that the Second
Republic, the Second Empire, the Franco-Prussian War and the Paris
Commune successively exacerbated.

Recent work has tended to locate the successful creation of a more
united French identity in the late nineteenth century during the Third
Republic. E.J. Hobsbawm (1983, pp.270–6) has seen the Republic as, after
1880, carrying out a profound exercise in social engineering by which a
secular primary education system sought to inculcate republicanism, and
governments inaugurated national festivals and encouraged the erection of
patriotic monuments. He distinguishes, however, between the rituals and
symbols of the Third Republic and those of the First, described above by
Hutchinson. This new republican imagery was generalized and vague and,
save for Bastille day, shied away from history. History prior to 1789 was
too monarchist and too Catholic, while the republican tradition was itself
fractured. Far safer to republicanize the normal pomp and ceremony of
state power, adorn it with the tricolour and accompany it with the Marseillaise, while the figure of Marianne, a female personification of the republican nation, was a suitably vague national icon and was reified in statues in
countless town squares. (Radical municipalities could demonstrate their
Jacobinism by having Marianne bare a breast, or even two; more moderate
republicans kept her fully clothed.)

The view that post-revolutionary France was inhabited by a nation of
French aware of their common nationality, sharing a common language and
common culture and bonded by a shared historic identity has been questioned more fundamentally by Eugene Weber in his influential study, *Peasants into Frenchmen; The Modernisation of Rural France, 1870–1914*, in
which, as the title suggests, he argues that most French country dwellers
and the inhabitants of small provincial towns did not think of themselves
as members of a French nation until the late nineteenth and early twentieth centuries. Localism still reigned supreme with people living physically,
culturally and psychologically within the world of their village. Far from
seeing themselves as French most did not even have a sense of regional
identity.

The making of the French state and the French nation can appear a bit like that historical chestnut, the almost proverbial rise of the middle class: historians are always discovering it in various centuries only for others to have to come along and discover it happening in a later period. The distinguished historian Marc Bloch argued for a French national consciousness existing as early as 1100, others have seen its development in the later Middle Ages, a considerable number have seen the 'absolute monarchy' of Louis XIV as completing the process, while numerous late modern historians and historians of nationalism have considered that the Revolutionary and Napoleonic periods made France a modern nation-state. What had happened, Weber argued, was that the consciousness of élite minorities of belonging to a nation had obscured from historians the fact that the illiterate or barely literate peasantry did not. It was only during the Third Republic that a combination of conscription into the army and a mass education system produced a more or less uniform national consciousness.

The continuity or change polarity which is at the heart of so much historical debate is perhaps really a spectrum, and for change to be seen to be accomplished depends much on the tightness of the definition of the supposed change and the rigour of the test of it. If for French national consciousness to exist the majority of the inhabitants of France must share it, then, perhaps, it was not developed until the late nineteenth century. If it is sufficient for an aristocratic élite to have an ethnic identity and to incorporate this into an administrative framework over at least northern France, then perhaps we can find it in the Capetian kingdom. If a national feeling among the propertied and the educated is the threshold then it can be discerned from the Revolution and during the first half of the nineteenth century. How many people must see themselves as belonging to the nation for the nation to exist: an élite, educated society or the masses?

Anthony Smith puts the case for the gradual development of French national feeling when he argues that:

> ... an originally Frankish ruling class *ethnie* managed, after many vicissitudes to establish a relatively efficient and centralized royal administration over northern and central France (later southern France). So it became able to furnish those 'civic' elements of compact territory, unified economy, and legal and civic standardization that from the seventeenth century onwards spurred the formation of the French nation as we know it. The process, however, was not complete until the end of the nineteenth century. Many regions retained their local character, even after the French Revolution. It required the application of Jacobin nationalism to mass education and conscription under the Third Republic to turn, in Eugene Weber's well-known phrase 'peasants into Frenchmen'. (Smith, 1989, pp.351–2)

Many of the peasants who became Frenchmen were, it must be remembered, Bretons, Alsatians or Gascons, and a characteristic of growing French national feeling was that it was expansive in that it sought to encompass other traditions. As the concept of a French citizen was not an inherently ethnic concept but always involved the idea of voluntarily wishing to be part of the nation this was not a matter of oppressing or subjugating Bretons or Flemmings but rather of including them. In what may be considered the period of liberal nationalism, (a rational progressive kind of nationalism in his view), E.J. Hobsbawm argues, national movements were movements for unification and the unified state was expected to have the characteristics of viable size, culturally and economically, and was unlikely to be entirely ethnically or linguistically homogenous. He quotes that epitome of nineteenth-century liberalism, J.S. Mill:

> Nobody can suppose that it is not more beneficial for a Breton or a Basque of French Navarre to be ... a member of the French nationality admitted on equal terms to all the privileges of French citizenship ... than to sulk on his own rocks, the half-savage relic of past times, revolving in his own little mental orbit, without participation or interest in the general movement of the world. The same remark applies to the Scottish highlander or Welshman as members of the British nation. (Hobsbawm, 1990, p.34)

But as Hobsbawm goes on to point out:

> ... there was nothing chauvinist in such a general attitude. It did not imply any hostility to the language and culture of such collective victims to the laws of progress (as they would certainly have been called then). On the contrary where the supremacy of the state-nationality and the state language were not an issue, the major nation could cherish and foster the dialects and lesser languages within it, the historic and folkloric traditions of the lesser communities it contained, if only as proof of the range of colours on its macro-national palette. (Hobsbawm, 1990, p.35)

This was because the dominant concept of French nationality and, as we shall see of British nationality, was not a racial or even largely an ethnic concept. The French language was not seen as a determinant of nationality, though to speak it was seen as proof of the acceptance of French identity.

When under the Third Republic a neo-Jacobin view of French identity was deliberately promulgated by radical governments, it was met by a very different blood and soil nationalism able to compete with it for mass support. This right-wing nationalism was in many respects radical rather than conservative. The protracted Dreyfus Affair which preoccupied France from 1894 to 1906 revealed deep divides in French society between those who believed the Jewish army officer, Captain Albert Dreyfus, innocent of spying and those who thought him guilty: on the one had the republican and anti-clerical Dreyfusards and on the other the clerical, right-wing anti-Dreyfusards. In 1899 Charles Maurras founded *Action Française*, promoting a mystical, nationalist, monarchist and anti-semitic programme. 'What is it that makes a man a Frenchman' asked Charles Maurras. 'The dead...The living expression of French nationalism is the result of the origin of its good and pure blood that we have received from our fathers and mothers'. French identity continued to be contested territory.

Britain

Britain and France together provided the main models for the liberal nation-state that was not based on ethnicity and where language was a pragmatic means of unification rather than being, in the sense it was used by Herder, the test by which the nation is known to exist. Britain was a special instance in that, within a century of the Act of Union of 1707, a sense of Britishness had been created that was superimposed on but coexisted with consciousness of English, Scottish and, indeed, with a continuing Welsh identity that had survived the earlier union of 1536.

Linda Colley (1992) in her study of the creation of a British identity in the eighteenth and early nineteenth centuries argues that, on one level Britain was much like the Trinity, 'both three and one, and altogether something of a mystery', while at another the strength of local and regional attachments made for layers of identity which were often uncertainly English, Scottish or Welsh, never mind British. Another way of looking at it is that Britain was a state, rather than a national, identity but a state identity that over time became a second national identity especially when looking outward rather than inward.

The national identities were complex both in themselves and in relation to each other. They depended little upon ethnicity. England and lowland Scotland had much the same ethnic composition and, indeed, northern England and the Scottish lowlands were identical in their Norse-Saxon mix. In language, culture, religion and ethnicity lowland and highland Scotland had little in common and lowlanders had traditionally a poor opinion of highlanders seeing them, as Linda Colley (1992, p.15) puts it, '… as members of a different and inferior race, violent, treacherous, poverty-stricken and backward'. Scottish national identity had to a considerable degree been developed in wars with England, though the history of the borders tends to contradict the view that border peoples develop a strong nationalism because of frequent skirmishing. English and Scottish borderers had for long shown a great willingness to raid and kill each other but exhibited, what was from the viewpoint of national governments, a regrettable tendency to band together and fall upon whatever national army lost. After the Union, although Scottish MPs and peers sat in the Westminster Parliament and Scots paid the same taxes as the English, Scotland retained its own Church and its own legal and educational systems, which made it nationally distinct beyond any region of France. What brought about the union was not ethnicity but rather a common monarchical allegiance, a common Protestantism and economic advantage. What built up the new sense of a dual British identity was those same monarchical and religious allegiances made firmer by prosperity and success in war.

Wales was institutionally indistinct from England but some three-quarters of the Welsh spoke the Welsh language, English in the eighteenth century being largely confined to border counties and the emerging urban centres. The sharp north–south divide made by the central mountain range meant that Wales had little internal cohesion, the north and south having much more contact with England than with each other. If England too exhibited considerable variety in terms of culture, customs and outlook, the main force which had created an English identity had been a centralized monarchy, consolidated and extended to Wales in the Tudor period, and the uniform law and national institutions it provided. It was this as well as its greater population, preponderant economic strength and favourable geographic position which made England the dominant and centralizing force in Britain. Among the factors that enabled a sense of British identity to emerge was the inter-marriage among the English and Scottish aristocracies which led to what was by the end of the century a British aristocracy. A liberal economy not only provided prosperity but led to economic unity and the steady integration of the landowning, professional and commercial classes within a British economy and culture. A series of wars with France provided a further focus of unity given greater force in that the enemy was Catholic.

It was again the antagonistic relationship with France that led to changes in the nature of British identity during the French revolutionary and Napoleonic Wars. In conscious contrast to France, British national feeling acquired a conservative character. The institutions of the monarchy had already been considerably refurbished and its popular appeal increased before the French Revolution but opposition to revolutionary France saw the evolution of a conscious and nationalistic British patriotism which identified the king as its focus and symbol. The emerging identification of the state with the nation, and patriotism with nationalism and monarchism found expression in major national festivals and ceremonies of thanksgiving for victories which were in part a riposte to the ceremonies of the Republic and Empire in France: the 'Great Service of National Thanksgiving' at St Paul's in 1797 to celebrate naval victories, Nelson's state funeral and the peace and victory celebrations of 1814. The celebration of George III's Jubilee foreshadowed those of Queen Victoria and in the parades of militia, the sermons in churches and cathedrals, and the dinner given to the poor which took place all over Britain, we find a celebration not just of the monarchy but of the nation, the one closely entwined with the other.

The English language was obviously of great importance in supporting the cohesion of the British state but there was little of that identification of language and ethnicity which we find in much of Europe. Just as the concept of being English owed much to culture and little to blood (Defoe had openly avowed the mongrel nature of the English in his *The Trueborn Englishman* in the early eighteenth century), the English were, as Hobsbawm (1990, p.109) puts it, '... quite exceptional in the nineteenth century ... in glorifying in the philological nature of their language'.

Britain had a problem when it came to that romantic interest in folklore and folk custom which became an almost essential corollary of national identity in the nineteenth century. As a new development Britain could only clothe itself in the past by going back to pre-Roman times while, in that England and most of Scotland and Wales were modern societies with largely liberal economies and relatively open social structures, folk customs and culture were much eroded. Most significantly the British nationalities lacked peasantries and therefore they lacked national dress and had to research and invent many of the romantic and mystic trappings of national identity.

Scottish lowlanders had to turn to the hitherto despised highland legacy and, as that was inadequate in itself, tartanize their national image with the help of imagination and straightforward forgery. The highly successful launch of the new identity took place ironically in the centre of the northern Enlightenment, Edinburgh, with the visit of the stout George IV, resplendent in the newly invented national costume and pink tights. The enthusiasm of Queen Victoria and Albert for the highlands helped further to superimpose kilt, sporran and glen upon the land of Adam Smith and David Hume.

The Welsh managed to find a national dress in some rather cut-off villages where the female inhabitants being old-fashioned were still wearing the tall hats and cloaks that had been the standard dress in most of Wales and England in the seventeenth century. Otherwise the Druids and the rediscovery of Celticism provided fertile sources for those engaged in what Prys Morgan (1983) has called 'the hunt for the Welsh past'. The resultant imagery entwined oddly with the modern dynamic of Welsh identity, non-conformity.

The English found things more difficult. For all the cult of Merrie England so dear to the Victorian imagination, and all the work of anti-quarians and collectors of folk songs, the folk tradition proved too varied, too remote and too quaint to adorn national identity. The nearest thing to peasant attire was the smock worn by many rural labourers but that was rather boring and the white shirts, knee-breeches and thick stockings of Morris dancers were the best invention could come up with.

The nineteenth-century British state was a largely unitary state, with the exception of Scotland's continued legal and educational differences. It presented the paradox or compromise of a standardized framework and strong local influence, relying as it did on unpaid country gentlemen and urban worthies to carry out so many administrative and judicial functions. It was, also, perhaps the most liberal state there has ever been, though, as, after 1867, it became more democratic, it became less liberal and state power increased. The line between civil society and the state was drawn differently from most European countries. Many of its major institutions, the prestigious schools and the universities for instance, were part of civil society rather than the state. The monarchy helped to distance the state from areas of life it controlled elsewhere, for as it lost political power, its patronage of institutions and societies protected pluralism and voluntarism from the state. What was to modern eyes the corrupt nepotistic 'fiscal–military state' of the eighteenth century evolved into the more meritocratic, exam-oriented administrative system of the late nineteenth century without any real clash between the aristocracy and the professional classes, the state absorbing the professionals rather than being redefined by them. It was a limited state, only moving fully into the elementary educational sphere in 1870 and abstaining from that essential characteristic of most European states, a conscript army.

If both Britain and France have been seen as state-nations, the state structure being the vehicle by which a more cohesive nation was formed, this was far less true in the case of Britain.

We have been concerned in the above sections with France and *Britain*, not the United Kingdom of Great Britain and Ireland but we must briefly consider the course of that later unsuccessful union. Although England had maintained an uncertain control over Ireland since the later middle ages, it was only integrated into the United Kingdom in 1801. The course of Irish nationalism exhibits a profound discontinuity, demonstrating in its different phases almost every variety of national separateness, political, economic, religious and cultural. From the efforts of the minority Protestant ascendancy to maintain its parliamentary independence from Westminster to the rise of Sinn Fein in the early twentieth century, Irish national movements were alternatively secular revolutionary (United Ireland), romantic revolutionary (Young Ireland), nationalist revolutionary (the Fenians and the Irish Republican brotherhood), peaceful single issue

(Catholic Emancipation), violent single issue (the Land League), constitutional nationalist (the Irish Parliamentary, or Home Rule Party) and cultural nationalist (the Gaelic League).

In relation to Ireland British governments were prepared, consciously and overtly, to use the power of the state to assist integration and to suppress or assuage discontent in a way they desisted from in Britain. Thus Ireland had a national police force, a Board of Commissioners for Education and a centralized, if rudimentary, health service while a succession of Land Acts dented the principles of private property to a degree unknown in Britain.

If Britain failed to integrate Ireland into the United Kingdom, Irish national movements failed to integrate Protestant Ireland. Cultural nationalism invigorated political nationalism and economic discontent but never disentangled itself from the religious, cultural and ethnic divide that had been laid down in the seventeenth century.

Exercise   List the differences you can discern between the following.

1   National identity.

2   The role of the state in promoting corporate identity in Britain and France.

Discussion   1   French national unity and to a degree identity had to surmount the very different images of France held by monarchists, Bonapartists and republicans and, though all accepted the nation, its character and historical identity were contested. The republican and to some extent the Bonapartist tradition imbued French identity with a radical hue while British identity and patriotism was more conservative and was focused on the monarchy.

The greater part of France had formed one kingdom since the early sixteenth century while Britain and Scotland had only been united since 1707.

Nevertheless very local and sub-regional identities may have been stronger in France than in Britain itself and the mass of the French peasantry only begun to see themselves as French in the late nineteenth century.

Both British and French identities were essentially inclusive rather than based on notions of birth or blood. If the British were subjects and the French citizens neither concept forbade new members. It was only in the late nineteenth century that the French catholic and monarchical tradition began to argue for a more racial concept of Frenchness.

2   Although British administration took place within a standard framework of law, its execution was largely in local hands and there was considerable licence for local power and initiative. France in contrast had a much more centralized administration. The French state had greater power and control than the British state. That power was used during the Third Republic in particular in the interests of the linguistic and cultural unity of the French people.

German and Italian nationalism

The creations of the Kingdom of Italy and the German Empire were the two great success stories for the principle of nationalism in the nineteenth century. As Anderson (p.224) comments, whereas in France, Britain and most of northern Europe, nationalism was a consolidating force: 'In Germany and Italy, on the other hand, it gave birth to great new states, though in each the work of unification was in the main controlled by men who were not nationalists'.

Exercise From your reading of Anderson, particularly Chapter 4, you should be able to answer the following questions:

1 How did the Vienna Settlement leave the geo-political maps of Germany and Italy?

2 How much enthusiasm for nationalism was there in either country at this time?

3 Who were the 'men who were not nationalists' who Anderson sees as in the main controlling the process of unification?

Specimen Answers

1 In the eighteenth century Germany had consisted of some three hundred states, many of them tiny, all of them, including Prussia, still technically part of the Holy Roman Empire presided over by the Habsburg dynasty. The Empire was abolished in 1806 and the German Confederation, established in 1815, consisted of thirty-nine states, including Austria as well as Prussia. The confederation was the only all-German institution but it was a loose arrangement under permanent Austrian chairmanship and Prince Metternich was able to use the Diet at Frankfurt, where the representatives of the states met, to thwart national and liberal aspirations.

Italy, after the Vienna Settlement, consisted of ten political units: two kingdoms, Sardinia (Sardinia and Piedmont) and the Two Sicilies (Sicily and Naples); the Duchies of Parma, Modena, Massa and Carrara and, until 1847, the Duchy of Lucca and the rather more important Grand Duchy of Tuscany; the Papal States; and Lombardy and Venetia which were part of the Austrian Empire.

2 Not very much according to Anderson. He argues that only a small educated minority in either country was attracted to the concept of nationalism. Very few Germans wanted anything more than a loose confederation akin to a rather stronger Holy Roman Empire while, 'The ordinary Italian was almost as far as he had ever been from envisaging or desiring national unity'.

3 One assumes that here Anderson is referring to Count Otto von Bismarck and Count Camillo Benso di Cavour. Certainly Bismarck had been opposed to the liberal-nationalism of the first half of the century while Cavour's main aim was the expansion of the power of Piedmont.

Despite the lack of popular enthusiasm for national unity and the hostility of rulers, governments and most of the nobility, there were certain factors favourable to Italian and German nationalism.

We have already considered the trends in German philosophic thought that stimulated enthusiasm for state and nation. Such thinking was not entirely separate from international and political developments. Hegel praised Napoleon for abolishing petty German states and felt that larger states with efficient bureaucracies and large armies were the pattern of the future and could best govern in the general interest. On the other hand the Napoleonic hegemony fanned both German and Italian national feeling. Fichte argued that France had forfeited her role as the standard bearer of liberty and that from henceforth it was the uncorrupted German nation and German culture that would defend freedom and provide the creative and spiritual force in European culture while Count Vittorio Alfieri in *Misogallo* (1804) called upon Italians to look upon hatred of the French as the means of uniting the Italian nation.

Eric Hobsbawm (1990) has argued that in the era of liberal nationalism during the first half of the nineteenth century, nationalism was regarded as essentially a progressive and modernizing force but that there were several criteria that a nation had to meet if it was to be able to be classed as a proper nation able to claim a nation-state. There was a 'threshold' that depended upon size and economic and military viability but which also involved an accepted historic tradition and a long established élite culture with a language that could become a national language. Italy and Germany passed the threshold with ease.

There is a degree of symmetry in the unification of Italy and of Germany. Despite the great differences between the north and south of Italy and the considerable divisions within Germany, in which religion played a large part, and despite the many *caveats* one must make in referring to tradition, history, culture and language, both were accepted entities, if not political entities.

In both the broad tendency was for liberalism and nationalism to go hand in hand until after mid-century but there were always different and competing nationalist agendas. In Italy three strands can be discerned: a radical, at times almost socialist, movement, which was secular and anti-monarchist and envisaged an Italian Republic; a Catholic movement, which saw in the Pope a focus for unity; and those who looked to the Piedmontese monarchy to take the leading role in unification. Amongst supporters of German unification there was the division between those who favoured the *Grossdeutsch* solution which would have included Austria and those who favoured a *Kleindeutsch* which would exclude her while, as Richard Bessel demonstrates in Unit 15, the growth of Prussian economic power meant that, despite the hostility of many liberals, Prussia increasingly appeared the natural leader of a new Germany.

The revolutions of 1848 had a common significance in Italy and Germany in promoting national unity and yet demonstrating the implausibility of revolution as a means of achieving it. If Mazzini (see Anderson pp.210–11) was the hero of Italian nationalism in 1848, it was the expansion of the moderately liberal Piedmont which appeared thereafter the best vehicle for the realization of a united Italy. In Germany the indecisiveness of the liberal-dominated Frankfurt Parliament and its recourse to the Prussian army for the war with Denmark, similarly discredited nationalism from below and enhanced the claims of a strong power, Prussia.

A major obstacle to both Italian and German unification was the Austrian Empire, which ruled northern Italy and was itself a German state. This obstacle was dealt with by judicious alliances in the Italian case and successful war in the German instance.

The joker in the pack in these twin processes of unification was Emperor Napoleon III and his role provides a warning against seeing the outcome as necessarily the outcome of deep historic forces. The complex and in the end unsuccessful diplomatic machinations of Napoleon III did much to promote, wittingly only in the case of Italy, the shape of Europe after 1870.

This symmetry should not be pushed too far for, as Unit 15 shows, the economic dimensions of Italian and German unifications were anything but symmetrical. Once in place however the arrival of two new nation-states, both representing dominant cultures and languages with long-standing historical associations, seemed both natural and stabilizing. If in Britain and France, where the nation had developed from the state, national feeling could be seen as a consolidating force, then in Italy and Germany where in part the national idea had created the state and in part one state expanded to fulfil the national ambition, the new order represented a process of concentration.

It is necessary to emphasize that neither unification had been the dream or achievement of the great mass of the populations. The new nation-states had been the dream of a small professional and educated minority and they had been created by diplomats and generals. A number of factors dictated that, in the late nineteenth century, nationalism became a concern of the mass of the population. Governments within nation-states used the administrative resources of the state to promote national feeling, increased literacy and a popular press made for national consciousness and whatever the extent of their electorates governments increasingly needed the support and consent of the mass of the population. One may conclude with Hobsbawm that for nationalism it was with mass society and democracy that the rot set in and nationalism became more populist, more chauvinistic and more racial. Nationalism and liberalism which had seemed to go hand in hand in for the first half of the century parted company.

The Habsburg Empire

If nationalism was a force for consolidation in Britain and France and for concentration in Italy and Germany, it was as Anderson (p.224) argues in eastern Europe, '...in the main a politically divisive force'. There is no better example of this than the Habsburg Empire.

The Europe re-drawn by the Vienna settlement was, like eighteenth-century Europe, a community of states but not of nation-states. In that the diplomats who met in Vienna were concerned to preserve monarchical legitimacy and buttress its restoration against revolution, their prime aims were to ward off liberalism and nationalism, then seen as complementary. Therein, claimed late nineteenth-century historians, lay their mistake. Later historians aware that the Versailles Settlement had been imbued with the spirit of national self-determination and mindful of its consequences have not been so sure that they were mistaken. Seen from a post-1945 viewpoint the unification of Germany can be seen to have profoundly upset the European balance of power while the national aspirations of east and central Europe played a central part in the origins of both the First and Second World Wars. While many in the late nineteenth and early twentieth centuries accepted the thesis that the frustrations of nationalist sentiment were a cause of instability, we can but observe the considerable stability that a multi-national state like the Habsburg Empire maintained for so long.

The distinctive feature of east and much of central Europe is its multiplicity of ethnic groups, the descendants of successive waves of migrations and invasions from central Asia: Huns, Avars, Slavs, Magyars and Turks. Too many nationalities, none of them living in geographically discreet areas for the concept of the nation-state to be realized without a constant battle for contested territories and a perpetual cavalcade of oppressors and oppressed.

No state was more threatened by the force of nationalism than the Habsburg Empire for, not only was it multi-national, but no one nationality was numerous enough to be entirely dominant. The capital of the Empire was Vienna and Germans and the German language were at the top of the hierarchy of nationalities (and/or ethnic groups) and languages, but the Empire would have been ungovernable without some recognition of the rights of other nationalities and languages. The cement that held the Empire together was loyalty to the dynasty and the dynastic state.

Exercise   List as many nationalities or ethnic groups living in the Empire in 1815 as you can think of.

Discussion   I expect you came up with some of the following: Germans, Magyars (Hungarians), Italians, Czechs, Slovaks, Poles and Croats. One could add Romanians, Ruthenians, Slovenes and Jews and there were other smaller groups of peoples.

The proportions of the population they formed were, out of the 51 million population in 1910 (after the Italian provinces of Lombardy and Venetia had been lost and after the incorporation of Bosnia-Herzecovina), as follows:

Germans 23.9%, Magyars 20.2%, Czechs 12.5%, Poles 10.8%, Ruthenians 7.9%, Rumanians 6.4%, Croats 5.3%, Slovaks 3.8%, Serbs 3.8%, Slovenes 2.6%, others (incl. Italians) 3.5%.

Jews are not included in this list but a list of religious affiliations gives Roman Catholic (including Uniate) 77.2%, Protestant 8.9%, Orthodox 8.9%, Jewish 3.9% and Muslim 1.1%, (Pearson, 1987).

As we have seen, however, ethnicity or nationality was not the sole or even the most important source of self-identification prior to the development of modern nationalism.

Exercise   1   What factors do you think were important in giving individuals an identity prior to the emergence of national feeling?

2   What factors do you think made for the growth of national feeling? (Think back to the summary of the views of some historians and sociologists with which we began this unit.)

Specimen Answers   1   Belonging to a particular village or locality was what mattered to the mass of the peasantry.

One's place in the social hierarchy, whether one was a peasant, a townsman or a member of the gentry or nobility. Religion was of great importance: whether one was a Catholic, a member of the Orthodox Church, a Uniate, a Lutheran or a Jew.

Loyalty to the Emperor or the dynasty should not be underestimated either.

2   There are the two kinds of pre-modern national feeling discerned by Anthony D. Smith: that felt largely by ruling groups and a popular ethnic identity. Some aristocracies were already in the early nineteenth century imbued with a sense of nationalism. The Polish, Magyar and Croatian aristocracies had collective aspirations which could over time transmit themselves to other classes. Alternatively a nationalism from below could build upon popular ethnic identity and develop in the context of urbanization, the spread of literacy and the emergence of groups of professionals.

A top-down process of nationalism which spread from aristocracies to peasantries did occur but was a slow process. When the Polish aristocracy revolted in 1846, the peasantry in Galicia turned on them and massacred two thousand of them. It was said that a Croatian noble would have as soon considered his horse a fellow Croatian as a Croatian peasant. It should be remembered though that these aristocracies included, what would have been in England, gentry and they were a sizeable proportion of the population. There is, nevertheless, an important distinction to be made between those nationalities who had native aristocracies, like the Magyars, the Poles and the Croatians, and those, like the Czechs, Serbs and Slovaks, who did not.

Urbanization increased the number of townspeople, not merely of artisans but of the middling and professional groups. Many townspeople would identify with the existing state and some would hope to gain employment in its service but others if they belonged to minority linguistic groups, might resent the dominance of another language and find that they had to learn it to gain advancement. The growth of towns brought in people from the surrounding countryside who might be Czech, Slovak or Polish where the urban population was German or Jewish. Thus Prague was a German-speaking city at the beginning of the century and Czech speaking by its end.

The growth of literacy, especially literacy in the national or vernacular language was a major development. Karl Marx referred, disparagingly

vernacular =

to the Slavs and other east central European peoples as 'peoples without history' but, as their languages became standardized and grammars were compiled, the writing of histories proceeded apace, almost always patriotic, usually embroidered and often containing invention. Anderson (p.212) comments that, '…in central and eastern Europe, [historical writing] tended to become largely the story of national rivalries'. The coming of books and newspapers in hitherto peasant languages greatly increased national consciousness.

The importance of religion in central and east European nationalism seems rather to contradict the view that nationalism is an inherently secular force designed to supplant older more cosmopolitan loyalties for religion often defined national identity. A major fault line has run across eastern Europe since the time of the division of the Roman Empire into its eastern and western components and the consequent division between Orthodox and Catholic Europe. The Catholicism of Poland and Croatia is as intrinsic to their identity as is the Orthodox faith to that of Serbia, while the parallel divide between Cyrillic and Roman scripts also helped ensure that modern nationalism would divide the Slavs.

It would be a great mistake to see the impact of the increased national consciousness of its peoples as having doomed the Habsburg Empire. Let us remind ourselves that it lasted until 1918 and that it took an enormous European upheaval to tear it apart. It survived the tremors of 1848 intact, only lost its main Italian possessions because of defeat at the hands of major powers and advanced further into the Balkans with the acquisition of Bosnia-Herzecovina. As Anderson comments, it found in *Kaisertreue*, 'personal loyalty to the emperor and the Habsburg family, a force which more than anything else held the empire together until 1918'. If the empire could not by its nature aspire to the historicist legitimacy of nationalism, it managed to build a formidable state machine and the works of the late nineteenth- and early twentieth-century novelists Robert Musil and Franz Kafka testify to the ubiquity of its bureaucracy.

Two major developments changed the nature of the empire and its problems. One was the rise of German nationalism and the eventual welding of the German states into a Prussian-dominated empire. The other was the slow collapse of the Ottoman Empire and the gaining of independence by its erstwhile subject peoples, the Serbs and the Romanians, on the other side of the Austrian Empire's borders. The Habsburg or Austrian Empire of the early nineteenth century had essentially looked west while at the same time it safeguarded the border between Christian Europe and the Ottoman Empire. The end of the Holy Roman Empire did not mean that the Habsburgs gave up their traditional role as the leaders of the German states, and they sought until 1866 to vie with Prussia for that leadership. Defeat in the Austro-Prussian War and the small Germany solution to German unification tilted the empire eastwards. The *Augsleich* or compromise of 1867 inaugurated a dual monarchy in which a German dominated Austria/Cisleithania shared control of the empire with a Magyar dominated Hungary/Transleithania. Once the possibility of a centralized and German-dominated empire had gone the monarchy had two main options, a tripartite empire which brought in the Slavs as a third partner or the oppression of the Slavs in conjunction with the Magyars. The choice of the latter option, the sharing of power with the most formidable nationalist entity that had only been subjugated with the help of Russia in 1849 had a wider than a purely domestic significance; it was by implication anti-Russian in that Russia saw herself as the protector of the Slavs.

The *Augsleich* sacrificed the most loyal subjects of the Habsburgs, the Croats who had stood by the empire in 1848, to the most rebellious, the Magyars. It also marked the end of any claim that the empire treated all its subjects equally. The Croats, who looked back to the historic kingdom of Croatia-Slavonia-Dalmatia and to the more recent Napoleonic province of Illyria, were to enjoy only the most limited autonomy under Magyar hegemony, while the Slovaks were subject to a systematic campaign to persuade them to become Hungarians: their schools were closed and their cultural associations disbanded while to enter the civil service it was necessary to speak the state language, Magyar.

Within the Austrian half of the state, the Germans refused at first to make concessions to Czech national feeling. The Czechs had increasingly migrated to the towns and in doing so, changed the composition of the urban populace from German and Jewish to Czech. There had not, since the battle of the White Mountain in the seventeenth century, been a Czech nobility which meant that Czech nationalism had a peaceful and rather middle-class character. It tended to be at first more a cultural than a political nationalism. Palacky's history placed great stress on the Protestantism of Jan Huss which had formed the basis of Bohemia's seventeenth-century revolt which sat oddly on a people which was now overwhelmingly Catholic. As with many national movements music played a part, Smetana and Dvorak replacing Mozart as the population of Prague changed from German to Czech. Immediately after the *Augsleich* the German minority retained control of the Bohemian Diet while the language of teaching in secondary schools and universities remained German but in 1880 the Czech language achieved equality with German in the lower levels of the administration and a Czech section was opened in Prague University.

It was the south Slav question, however, that was to give the dual monarchy its greatest problems. Taylor (1954, p.228) wrote a propos the revolt of the Christian Slavs of Bosnia-Herzecovina against their Turkish rulers and fellow Slav Muslim landlords (today's 'Bosnians'), which was followed by a Serbian declaration of war against the Ottomans, that, 'Once the Balkan Slavs were astir, the Russian government dare not let them fail; Austria-Hungary dared not let them succeed'. But the real problem was not any desire of the empire's Slavs for independence, let alone union with Serbia, which they regarded as a wild and uncivilized country, but the refusal of the Hungarians to compromise with Slav national feeling. It was Magyar obstinacy which made it appear that the Slavs were a threat to the empire and led to the forward policy in the Balkans which saw Austria-Hungary given control but not sovereignty over Bosnia-Herzecovina by the Treaty of Berlin of 1878. The acquisition of another million or so Slavs was an odd way to solve the empire's Slav problem.

Until the assassination of the pro-Slav Franz-Ferdinand in 1914 by the Serb Gavril Principio (an event which was quickly followed by the burning of Serbian property in Sarajevo by the Bosnian Muslims, who were quite happy with Austro-Hungarian rule), Hungarian opposition thwarted those who favoured the plan which would have had the best chance of stabilizing the empire, the trialist solution which would have given the Croats and perhaps other Slavs a partnership with the Germans and Hungarians.

Exercise   Does the example of the Habsburg Empire and the previous discussion of France and Britain take you any further in answering the question with which we started this unit: is nationalism a modern development?

Discussion   Well, I'm not sure that I have an answer but I suppose I'd compromise and say that nationalism is a modern concept that calls upon ancient and basic feelings. It arose in the circumstances of that loose catch-all term modernization, which encompasses industrialization, urbanization, the extension of literacy and new means of communication and the clash between reason and romanticism in the wake of the French Revolution. But its very different characteristics in different places and circumstances, not just the distinction between national identity in the nation-state of France and the identities of the peoples of Austria-Hungary, but the differences between Hungarian and Czech nationalism, makes me think that modern nationalisms and states are substantially built on the framework of past cultures. With the help of a bit of invention of course.

References

Anderson, B. (1991), *Imagined Communities: Reflections on the Origin and Spread of Nationalism*, Verso, London.

Breuilly, J. (1982), *Nationalism and the State*, Manchester University Press, Manchester.

Clark, J.C.D. (1994), *The Language of Liberty, 1660–1832*, Cambridge University Press, Cambridge.

Colley, L. (1992), *Britons. Forging the Nation 1707–1837*, Yale University Press, New Haven.

Gellner, E. (1983), *Nations and Nationalism*, Basil Blackwell, Oxford.

Gellner, E. (1994), *Encounters with Nationalism*, Blackwell, Oxford.

Gildea, R. (1987), *Barricades and Borders, Europe 1800-1914*, Oxford University Press, Oxford.

Hobsbawm, E.J. (1990), *Nations and Nationalism since 1780*, Cambridge University Press, Cambridge.

Hobsbawm, E.J. and Ranger, T. (eds) (1983), *The Invention of Tradition*, Cambridge University Press, Cambridge.

Hutchinson, J. (1994), *Modern Nationalism*, Fontana, London.

Hutchinson, J. and Smith, A.D. (eds) (1995), *Nationalism*, Oxford University Press, Oxford.

Kedourie, E. (1967), *Nationalism*, Hutchinson, London.

Morgan, P. (1983), 'From a Death to a view: The Hunt for the Welsh Past: the Romantic Period' in Hobsbawm and Ranger (eds).

Pearson, R. (1987), *The Fontana Companion to European Nationalism 1789-1914*, Fontana, London.

Smith, A.D. (1971), *Theories of Nationalism*, Duckworth, London.

Smith, A.D. (1986), *The Ethnic Origins of Nations*, Blackwell, Oxford.

Smith, A.D. (1989), 'The Origins of Nations', *in Ethnic and Racial Studies*, Routledge and Kegan Paul, London.

Smith, A.D. (1991), *National Identity*, Penguin, London.

Taylor, A.J.P. (1954), *The Struggle for Mastery in Europe 1848–1918*, Clarendon Press, Oxford.

Weber, E. (1976), *Peasants into Frenchmen. The Modernisation of Rural France, 1870–1914*, Stanford University Press, Stanford, Calif.

Unit 13
Language, literacy and education

Prepared for the course team by Arthur Marwick

Contents

Study timetable

Weeks of study	Texts	Video	AC
1.5	Unit 13; Anderson, Documents III.1–3		

Aims

The aims of this unit are:

1   to introduce the significant aspects of, and the main developments in, language, literacy and education;

2   to present analyses of their relationships to each other and to state, economy and nation.

Objectives

By the end of this unit you should be able:

1   to explain the basic relationships between language (as the word is used in this course), literacy, and education;

2   to discuss in an informed way the relationships between, on one side, industrialization and economic growth, and, on the other, literacy and education;

3   to discuss in a balanced way education as a force for stability and the status quo, and education as a force for reform, democracy, and revolution;

4   to analyse in an informed way the relationships between education and the growth of the state, and between education and the development of different groups within the state, e.g. the professions, women, different social classes;

5   to explain and compare the different educational developments in the different European countries;

6   to discuss in an informed way the relationships between language, nationality, and the state;

7   to discuss intelligently the arguments about language as an instrument of power and language as an instrument of liberation;

8   to continue to develop your understanding of the nature of historical study and of historical sources.

How language, literacy, and education relate to each other

As you already know, almost all of the most important words in academic study tend to have a range of meanings: 'language' is one such word. Broadly, there is a distinction between, on the one hand, 'language' in a general sense, as when I and my colleagues tell students that in serious historical study it is vital to pay careful attention to the problems of 'language' (the way the same word has different meanings, the way certain words take on particular overtones, etc.), or when people talk about 'the language of film', or 'the language of architecture', and, on the other hand, 'language', in a specific sense (where one speaks of 'a language' – that is with the indefinite article, or of 'languages' in the plural), where 'language' is used to signify 'the system of words and sentences by which human beings belonging to the same "aggregate" (i.e. tribe, community, nation, etc.) communicate with each other'. In this second usage, which is the one I am concerned with in this unit, examples of 'languages' are: French, Flemish, Gaelic, Neopolitan, etc.

Is there a difference between 'language' and 'dialect'? It has famously been said (by the Toronto sociologist Gianrenzo Clivio), that 'Language is simply dialect with an army, navy and airforce', that is, that the system of speech which is 'successful', is adopted by the state and supported by it against the 'unsuccessful', alternative systems, is 'canonized' as a 'language', while the 'unsuccessful' systems are written off as mere 'dialects'. In so far as this aphorism draws attention to the social and political influences bearing on language development, it is very useful. But if not too clever by half, it is certainly a bit too clever.

Indisputably some languages are privileged, and some languages are spurned (part of what we have to study concerns the rise and fall of different languages, and the causes and consequences thereof). But they remain languages, that is distinct systems of speech. We shall attain greater precision if we reserve 'dialect' for 'minority or local variants of a language' (though, true enough, as nation-states form, what was majority can become minority, and what was local can become national). Italy presents a fascinating case. A tiny minority of educated people throughout the peninsula could communicate in a formal, literary, Italian which, through the genius of the poet Dante, author of the *Divine Comedy*, had emerged in Tuscany as early as the beginning of the fourteenth century. The illiterate, or ill-educated, majority spoke their own dialects – usually dialects of *Italian*, though Neopolitan, the language of the Kingdom of Naples, was closely related to Spanish, and there were Greek-speaking enclaves in the far South. Venetian (to choose an important example) was significantly different from literary (Tuscan) Italian; Sicilian was a separate language. The highly educated minority in Piedmont preferred to write and speak French, though some of them were bilingual in French and Italian; the illiterate or ill-educated spoke dialects of either Italian or French (see Hearder, 1994).

Being able to *speak* a language is a faculty derived from the long process of human evolution: *reading* and *writing* (broadly what I mean here by literacy) have to be learned. Human beings naturally speak their 'mother tongue', the language of those in their immediate environment (some human beings, relatively unusually, grow up speaking two tongues, i.e. they are bilingual like some of the educated in Piedmont). Other languages have to be learned. Reading and writing may be taught within the family, as recent research (by Furet and Ozouf, 1982; Maynes, 1985; Vincent, 1989) has increasingly brought out. It could be argued that older historians, with their obsession with schools as instruments of power and oppression, have exaggerated the influence of schooling (at this level probably a better word than 'education'). Arithmetic, the other basic element in what I shall be calling Elementary Education (the word 'primary' is only really appropriate when 'primary' automatically leads to secondary, which, it is most important to know, was very much not the case in the Europe we are studying), might be taught at home, but was more likely to require schooling. Elementary education would also usually contain religious instruction and aim at inculcating deference and respect for authority.

Schools could most certainly be an agency for inducting pupils into the language of a major imperial or state power, as distinct from their mother tongue: for example, Russian, or German, instead of Polish, French instead of Occidan (the language of Languedoc). The army (outside of Britain all males were liable to conscription) could also serve this function.

Educational systems differed in the different countries, and all expanded and changed rapidly in our period. Schools were run by the churches and by private individuals: intervention by the state was not necessarily the sole, or even essential, ingredient of educational change. Often the state was more concerned with élite institutions for training civil servants, army officers, and professionals (e.g. engineers, doctors and lawyers), than with what I shall call Popular Education. The structure of schooling was very closely related to social structure. Broadly, across Europe, it can be divided as follows:

Elementary Schools: two, three or four years for children of peasants and workers. During the century higher elementary schools were sometimes added.

Secondary Schools: these were mainly for the middling sort in small business or commerce or the minor professions; pupils often came through private schools rather than the ordinary primary schools (which, frankly, are best envisaged as leading to a dead end).

Grammar Schools (gymnasien in German, and the Russian variant; lycées, in French and the Italian variant) formed yet another separate route. In general they prepared the rich and the aspiring for universities or specialist higher education institutions. The pupils came through (often expensive) private 'preparatory schools'. In England certain prestigious grammar schools developed into very exclusive so-called 'public schools'.

This was an exaggerated form of a universal development: every country had its 'snob' schools, even though run by the state.

Technical Schools or 'modern' schools. Grammar school education was based on the classics (Latin and Ancient Greek). Somewhat stumblingly, states began establishing technical and science-based schools at various levels.

Universities and advanced professional institutions. These had grown up in the middle ages, but, under the Napoleonic impact, came to be seen in many countries as the state-sponsored controlling apex of the entire educational system.

Now, who taught the teachers? A crucial aspect of nineteenth-century educational reform was the establishment of teacher-training 'colleges' (the term is too grand), or 'normal schools' as they are much more usually known across Europe. Again there was strict social segregation. University and grammar school teachers went to university. Elementary school teachers (*instituteurs* in French) were almost invariably from humble backgrounds, proceeding through elementary school to normal school.

It is vital to have in mind a clear model of the class structure of education; but always remember that, even within countries, the systems, in reality, were very diverse, and developed in response to pressures other than those of the state (e.g. religion, private profit-making, consumer demand).

How far, and in what ways, language, literacy, and education affected, and were affected by, the development of state, economy, and nation

Simple, but far from utterly inaccurate, propositions might be as follows:

1   As literacy in specific privileged languages (e.g. Russian, German, French) increased (or was imposed) so the nation grew in strength, with minority groups being marginalized.

2   As states grew in strength and ambition, they saw the need to foster education at all levels, in order to:
    (a)   consolidate the sense of unified national identity;
    (b)   provide the skills necessary for economic growth;
    (c)   improve government and essential services (medicine, law, etc.).

3   Even for 'lesser nationalities', if, escaping the embrace of the great powers, they could develop literacy and education in their own language, they could enhance their claims to their own statehood.

Keep two points in mind:

1   The diversity of educational systems and of the pressures causing their development.

2   The point made in the introduction to this block that many ordinary people felt far greater loyalty to their immediate local community than to any distant and abstract notion of 'nation'.

Exercise   Turn to Anderson and read: pp.169 (beginning of new section) to p.176 (l.4. 'female teachers'), and p.181, beginning of last paragraph, 'The impetus behind...' to p.182 (end of section). After a couple of readings, attempt answers to the following questions:

1   Did industrialization foster or retard:
     (a)   the growth of literacy;
     (b)   the provision of education?

2   Is there a relationship between the expansion of education and economic growth?

3   Was education an agency of reform and revolution, or of stability and maintenance of the status quo? Is there a relationship between the expansion of democracy and the expansion of education?

4   Tease out the relationships between education and the growth of the professions, and between education and the rise of the state. What is the broad effect on class structure of the expansion of education?

5   Did the education of women create feminism, or did feminism create the education of women?

6   How would you summarize the main causes of, or motivations for, the main advances in education (as given by Anderson)? Rank them in order of importance. (Don't worry if there is some duplication of earlier answers.)

7   Tease out the relationships between language and nationalism.

8   Where does education fit into these relationships?

9   Which were the greater, the positive or the negative results of what Anderson calls 'linguistic nationalism'?

10   What are the interactions, and conflicts (if any), between educational expansion, religion, and 'culture' (another word which needs careful handling, but here can be taken as including literature, theatre, music, dictionaries, study of folklore, the press, and anything else you think relevant).

Specimen Answers and   1   Anderson suggests that the earlier stages of industrialization, together
Discussion   with the 'explosive' rise in population (which, as you know, is linked to industrialization, though not 'caused' by it; what it did cause was the influx into the towns), may have damaged literacy and provision of education (factories did not need 'well-educated workers' – an unsatisfactorily imprecise phrase, incidentally; schools could not cope with the increased numbers; parents thrust their children into the new source of income as early as possible). However, Anderson argues, the later stages of industrialization required literacy for clerical workers as well as technical training for operatives, thus creating pressure for universal elementary education. Though Anderson is a little vague, some of the points he makes could suggest that a need for secondary education was beginning to be felt in the later stages. This suggestion is reinforced when Anderson goes on to refer to the need 'for men to be able to understand price-lists or newspaper reports or instruction manuals' (p.170).

2   Anderson indicates that there *is* a relationship and that, as so often with such major historical questions, it is a two-way one. Economic development, as we have just seen, eventually required an expansion of education. But then expansion of education fostered economic growth: 'A literate population was likely to be a market-oriented population and therefore one which was progressing economically'. Note the comparative statistics for Sweden and Spain (pp.170–1) and the suggestion that a literacy rate of 30 to 40 per cent is needed for 'any significant breakthrough … to the greater wealth … offered by industrialization'.

3   In a really thoughtful answer one might begin by saying it depended on the kind of education, for, if you have read Anderson carefully you will have noted that he, as a historian, does not answer my first question on one side or the other. What he does is quote the contrasting views of influential people at the time: republicans and radicals thought mass education was essential if voters were to be enlightened enough to support them; conservatives thought education would encourage the masses to respect the forces of authority (try to fix the quotation from Guizot (p.170), at least approximately, in your memory – it is a classic). My own answer would be that the education (particularly the elementary education) that was actually provided served mainly to bolster the institutions and ideologies of the centralizing state, but that it did at least provide the basic skills through which workers could begin to think more systematically about their own grievances, and about issues of reform and revolution. I would think it beyond dispute that the major reform movements of the nineteenth century would not have been possible without the expansion of education; equally, education was undoubtedly a factor in increasing the strength and stability of the state. The relationship between democracy and education is clear: the arguments of the time were:

(a)   if you gave people the vote, you would have to educate them to ensure that they used it responsibly;

(b)   that you could not give people the vote until you were sure they were sufficiently educated.

4   I said 'tease out' because once again we have an interactive process, not a simple cause-and-effect one. Industrialization created both a general need for an expansion of education, and the beginnings of the new professional class. The creation of this class, in turn created a further demand for education; at the same time, without expanding educational provision the development of the professions would have been impossible. Expansion of education naturally entailed an expansion in the number of teachers: but we have to be careful here, in that a large proportion of elementary teachers, certainly for the major part of the nineteenth century, were working class in status, rather than part of the new professional class. Because they were educated (and, Anderson says, intelligent) the new professions were not just another class, but had special influence. A strong state needed a strong professional class (civil servants especially, obviously), while, in any case, the professionals, because of their education, were (influential) supporters of a strong state (using its powers in 'an enlightened and creative way'). The links between education and the state can be expressed as follows:

(a) the expansion of education depended upon action by a strong state;

(b) the strong state depended on a complaisant population and social stability: education was a factor in producing these;

(c) the strong state required an effective professional class, which in turn depended on there being adequate educational provision.

The main class point dealt with by Anderson is this one of the addition of a substantial (and influential) professional sector to the middle classes. Anderson also identifies higher education as a 'ladder' creating social mobility (but we can only be dealing with a tiny minority here; personally I'd have thought secondary education more important in this respect). Bringing together all the information we have, we could perhaps say that education served to make individual classes more homogeneous and to bring the different classes closer together, while at the same time stabilizing the broad lines of the class structure. Don't worry if you didn't make much headway with this part of the question, but reflect now on this very condensed summary I have just given.

5   Good question! The central factor identified by Anderson is the growth of the middle class (irrespective, it would seem, of the growth of education). Clearly, access of women to education helped to strengthen feminism, while the growth of feminism intensified the demand for women to have access to secondary and higher education. Good questions do not always have straightforward answers, but they may help us to tease out complex problems.

6   At the end of the section Anderson speaks of 'the reforming impulse' which he sees as part both of the growth of the humanitarian spirit in the nineteenth century, and as being calculated and selfish. He then refers again to education as forming an effective defence of existing society. But, in talking of 'motives' we must remember that many who wanted to change existing society were advocates of educational expansion. Ranking of 'causes' can be a slightly artificial activity, yet one must try to be analytical. I would do it this way:

(a) industrialization was fundamental to the spread of education;

(b) so too was the partly related, partly autonomous, expansion of the state;

(c) we then have a mixture of motivations as expressed by humanitarians, reformers and conservatives.

7   According to Anderson, the identification of a national language came to be seen as an indispensable component of nationalism; this fundamental fusion between nationalism and the (alleged) national language he terms 'linguistic nationalism'. Then, as the claims of a particular nationalism begin to be asserted, one language (even a 'mere peasant' dialect) is privileged while rival languages or dialects are suppressed.

8   Well, Anderson summarizes the process brilliantly in another of these sentences that it really is worthwhile trying to retain in your memory (foot of p.215): 'The growth of universal, or at least large-scale, primary education went during the century in step with the growth of

popular nationalism: the second could hardly have existed without the first'. But this is rhetoric, of course. Be sure you have digested the detailed points in the paragraph which runs from p.215 to p.216.

9   Let's look at both 'positive' and 'negative' in turn.

(A)   Positive
(i)   resurrected peasant dialects into refurbished languages;
(ii)   rediscovered forgotten literatures ('some of them of real value'! – one knows what Anderson means, but perhaps not too felicitously put);
(iii) impetus to study of national history and folklore;
(iv)   encouraged production of national dictionaries;
(v)   and construction of national theatres;
(vi)   largest element in 'general cultural nationalism', involving both great composers and collections of folk tunes;
(vii) created bridges between cosmopolitan high culture and local popular culture.

(B)   Negative
(i)   some of the cultural manifestations were 'ridiculous';
(ii)   ruling nations impeded the development of languages of subject ones;
(iii) schools might teach only the ruling language;
(iv)   the development of leaders among subject nationalities was impeded;
(v)   ambitious figures were forced to learn the ruling language;
(vi)   books in subject languages were suppressed.

This was an easy question. If you were unable to answer it adequately you must practise your skills in reading, and in deriving vital information from what you read.

10   Anderson says less about religion in relation to education than one might have expected. There are hints that at the beginning of our period most education was in the hands of religious bodies, and that these continued to be significant providers of education, and that there could be conflicts over education between religious and secular authorities (but this is not spelled out). On culture there are obvious comments to be made – without some basic level of education there is unlikely to be much demand for certain cultural artefacts, institutions and practices (e.g. novels, symphony concerts, art galleries). With the activities we have just been itemizing in the previous question the immediate connection is with nationalism, but then, as we learned in answering the question before that, education and this type of nationalism were intimately interrelated. Earlier (last sentence of my discussion of question (1)) we brought out the close interconnection between education and the rise of the press.

Literacy and education: A comparative study of various European countries

One of the dangers of having a course confined to nineteenth-century history is that of giving the impression that *all* major developments took place in that century. We cannot completely ignore the enduring influence of the Church, the effects of the sixteenth-century reformations, of the seventeenth-century scientific revolution, of the eighteenth-century Enlightenment, and of the French Revolution and its Napoleonic aftermath. Still more important, we cannot take the nineteenth century as a unified period. Not only do we have the 'backward', 'peripheral' countries, but large tracts of other countries remained only little affected by industrialization and urbanization. Most of the big reforms came only late in the century or in the first years of the new century. Furthermore, while industrialization is clearly the major structural force behind educational reform, we should beware of making industrialization a universal explainer. And we should particularly note the significance of consumer demand, neatly summed up in this statement by Victoria Brocker, working-class rebel of the Paris Commune, about her ambitions for her son:

> How many wonderful dreams I had for my dear child. I wanted him to go to school, to be well brought up, how happy I would have been if one day chance had smiled on me and my son would have become a doctor. (quoted in Maynes, 1985, p.144)

To get a broad comparative picture, basic statistics are invaluable.

Exercise   Look at Document III.3 and consider Tables 1, 2 and 3. Now attempt to answer the following questions.

1   Sort out the best and the worst countries with regard to (a) enrolment and/or attendance at elementary schools, and (b) literacy. How do the good records and the bad records relate to the power of the state, the nature of the economy, and the role of nationalism, in the particular countries? Do you notice any discrepancies between elementary school attendance and literacy? Can you explain them? (Don't worry if you can't immediately think of something.)

2   What do you think is the relevance of the number of postal deliveries per head? (Again don't worry if nothing occurs to you.)

Discussion   In this discussion I am going to take both questions together.
On the basis of one table only, Switzerland comes out very high on (a) and (b). Of the major countries Germany (which, of course, includes Prussia and Bavaria) comes out best. Austria does reasonably well on school attendance, but not outstandingly well on literacy. Britain is behind only Switzerland in literacy, but below Austria in school attendance. Sweden (singled out, remember, by Anderson) is, in 1850, relatively low on enrolment (same figure as Prussia in 1820), but by 1890 is doing well both on attendance and literacy. French school statistics show rapid improvement (an important point) and by 1890 are high on both counts, with literacy, however, on the low side. Belgium has lower school attendance, but higher

literacy, than Austria. Italy is pretty mediocre on all counts, while (on very inadequate statistical evidence – a revealing point in itself about these backward countries) Spain and Russia would seem, as it were, to be heading for relegation (or should I perhaps say 'revolution'?).

Switzerland is a fascinating case in suggesting the need for caution in applying our general propositions. Made up of three distinct linguistic communities (German, French and Italian) it is almost the reverse of a strong centralized state, and, although relatively prosperous, it is scarcely yet an industrialized state (I don't expect you necessarily to know these things: if you simply singled out Switzerland you were doing well). However the freedom of expression enjoyed by each linguistic community must, I am quite sure, be a factor in the high literacy rate (literacy here connotes literacy, not in one imposed national language, but in one's own mother tongue). We do, I think, have to recognize that Switzerland is an exceptional case, while the German figures do indeed suggest a strong correlation between a strong state, growing economy, and pronounced national identity, and education and literacy. The same comment could be made about France, with lower literacy figures being partly explained by the existence of non-French-speaking minorities within France. Britain presents the most obvious anomaly with respect to the correlation between schooling and literacy, indicating (what we know to be true) that the family element was strong in teaching literacy. It's here the postal statistics are significant: the British were literate, they wrote and read more letters than anyone else (the other point I'll just add in here, is that the British were very active newspaper readers). Belgium, you may recall, only achieved independence early in our period: perhaps we can (in part) attribute lowish attendance figures to the problems of a recently-formed state, and the decent literacy figure to fulfilled nationalism. Italy's problems you probably know: recently-established, weak central state, a variety of very distinctive dialects, poor economic record. Though long-established, Spain has these problems too, but more so. Autocratic government in Russia was good at stopping things, but not very good at achieving them: almost uniquely in Europe it actually feared providing education for the peasant masses.

I hope you had fun with that little exercise: my apologies if I have not covered all of the points you might well have made. It is interesting that all governments (even the most inefficient) kept statistics on the major government service of the day, the post. Historians have to use whatever sources are available. Statistics of literacy, it is important to be aware, are very largely based on marriage registers where one can identify the proportion of couples who still cannot sign their names.

Exercise   What does Table 2 tell us about the European education system's discrimination against females?

Discussion   Well (I hope you thought to note this), the source is confined to Paris in the 1870s, and to, roughly, elementary, higher elementary, and lower secondary education. For what it's worth, it does suggest that discrimination against girls was far from total, but that discrimination against them increased in the higher age groups. (In fact, I can tell you now, discrimination against females across Europe came very near to being total in higher-secondary, grammar-school, and university education.) I picked this table just to draw attention to an important issue (remember Anderson's points brought out in my very first exercise). Broadly, the Parisian situation was rather more favourable to girls than you would find anywhere else in Europe, outside of Germany.

To provide you with basic information necessary if you are to attempt TMA or exam questions relating to education, I'm going to give summaries of developments in the main countries. Boring, I fear, but unavoidable.

French governments were less consistently active in promoting education than were Prussian and German ones, but were more active than any of the other main countries, so I'm taking France as a kind of median case, handling the other countries more briefly. I draw heavily, but not exclusively, on the essays by Gontard (1982), Cauvin (1982), and Ravaglioli (1982).

France

Restoration France, 1815–30

In the spring of 1815, through the private initiative of aristocrats of both birth and wealth, who conceived elementary education as a vital defence against revolutionary madness, the Society for Elementary Education was established. From England (note again this kind of transnational influence), the Society imported the 'monitorial' system (a system whereby the bulk of the teaching was done by older pupils, a system which was nothing if not cheap), and by 1820 was running 1,300 schools. However the clergy resented this English (and, therefore, 'Protestant') influence, and in the 1820s the Society's schools declined, while those run by the clergy increased. At the same time the University (the primary agency of the state in the sphere of education) struggled to assert overall control over elementary education, first through a weak ordinance of 1816, then more firmly in 1828. Most important was the law of 1817 which granted men who signed up for ten years service as *instituteurs* (elementary teachers) – and it was service in the most servile and penurious conditions – exemption from military service (very revealing of how elementary education was perceived!). From Prussia (NB!) was imported the idea of setting up normal schools (teacher-training institutions of the most austere sort) in every department. Progress was slow, coverage was patchy, and standards abysmal.

The reforms of Guizot and after, 1830–48

Guizot is pronounced 'gee-zoh', so if I were chatting to you face-to-face, I'd make a little jest to help you memorize a vital point, along the lines of: 'Guizot is the geezer we met earlier (above, p.7), and whose justification for elementary education I suggested you memorize'. Guizot's law of June 1833 stipulated that every commune must have an elementary school, with lodgings and a minimum stipend of 200 francs for the *instituteur*, and every town a 'higher elementary school' (to serve the needs of commerce and industry); the establishment of normal schools in every department was made compulsory. It is possible to see the *instituteurs* as intended allies of the state against the influence of the local priests, though in fact Guizot made religious instruction compulsory and involved the clergy in the supervision of the schools. In 1836, take note!, all provisions were extended to girls. A General Manual of Elementary Instruction was issued in 1832, and centralized state control further emphasized in the creation of a corps of elementary inspectors in 1835. Boys at elementary school rose from 1,200,000 in 1832 to 2,178,000 in 1848; girls from 1,100,000 in 1837 to 1,354,000 in 1848 (obviously social and family resistances to educating girls remained stronger than the expressed wish of the state). The creation of higher elementary schools and of normal schools was impressive. According to Gontard (1982), however (you will remember our earlier discussion), many newly literate pupils took to reading revolutionary tracts as many *instituteurs* (resentful of their appalling conditions) became radicals and revolutionaries.

The 1848 revolution, the reaction, and the empire, 1851–79

Carnot proposed that elementary education be compulsory and free, but in the Reaction education regressed. The higher elementary schools were suppressed, normal schools were no longer obligatory, and the Falloux Law of March 1850 placed the *instituteurs* under the strict supervision of mayors and priests. Direct state control was tightened in 1854 when the *instituteurs* were placed under the control of the prefects. But the Italian war of 1859 (note how external events can influence social policy) altered Church/ State relations, and Louis Napoleon's government now started to withdraw education from Church influence. Statistics in 1863, demonstrating that out of four million children aged nine to thirteen, 900,000 were not at school, forced the minister responsible, Duruy, to propose (October 1864) free and compulsory elementary education. Conservative forces successfully opposed him, but the law of April 1867 empowered those communes which so wished to introduce free education. Under Duruy's reforms girls' secondary education began to develop.

The Third Republic 1870–1914

From 1879 onwards there was a burst of legislation, introduced by the Republican Minister, Jules Ferry, and, changing, in the words of Gontard, 'the face of elementary education': each department was required to maintain two normal schools, one male, one female (law of 1879); new, more advanced, higher elementary schools were established (law of 1880); teachers were required to have a training certificate, but were no longer to be subject to local church authority, and all elementary education was made free (laws of 1881), and then compulsory for all six-to-thirteen-year-olds, while religious education was replaced by 'civic and moral' instruction (law of 1882). Finally improved salaries and a proper career structure were introduced for *instituteurs*, with their exemption from military service being abolished. *Instituteurs* continued to be recruited from the peasant and working classes as well as from *instituteur* families but (one further demonstration of the relationship between education and class) can now be taken as forming a section of the lower middle class (mainly left-wing in outlook).

Recent research (by Furet and Ozouf, 1982) suggests that, because of high consumer demand, the comprehensive elementary system was actually largely in place *before* the Ferry reforms. A balanced account would stress *both* state initiatives and consumer demand.

Prussia/Germany

As products of the eighteenth-century Enlightenment (though also strongly tinged by Protestantism), there were in Prussia: a compulsory national system of (elementary) folk schools (consolidated in 1794), a national secondary education exam (instituted 1788), several higher elementary schools, and a network of normal schools. At the beginning of the nineteenth century, one very specific impetus to educational reform was the shock of defeat by the Napoleonic armies. While a wide-ranging general reform programme was put in place (notably in the army – once again there appears to be an association between national power and education) the distinguished liberal intellectual, Wilhelm von Humboldt, appointed Minister of Education in 1809, determined on wholesale reform of secondary and university education, based on the principles of Greek humanism (nothing very 'industrial' about this!). Prussia was equipped with a system of high-quality grammar schools (singular, *gymnasium*; plural, *gymnasien*) designed to prepare boys for university entrance. As the historic university of Halle was now stranded in Napoleonic Westphalia, in 1810 the new university of Berlin was founded (throughout the rest of the century profoundly influencing philosophy, religion, education, science, and historical method throughout Europe and North America). German education was to have powerful international effects, but was also deeply nationalistic: the philosopher J.G.Fichte, author of *Addresses to the German Nation* (1807–8), 'saw Germany as increasingly unified by aggressive national educational systems and by the traditions and ambitions of a common culture' (Gay and Webb, 1973, p.528); and von Humboldt, as Anderson tells us (p.210) 'came at last to believe that "there are only two realities, God and the nation" '. In general, throughout the entire period, German teachers were more conformist than French ones.

After 1815 German thinkers continued to lead in the field of educational theory, but the system began to stagnate, with the Protestant clergy reasserting their control over it. Elementary teachers, and also Diesterweg, director of the Berlin Normal School, were prominent in the events of 1848, when attempts were made to free the schools from religious control, and to establish single schools combining primary and secondary study. Reaction followed, and the notorious Stiehl regulations of 1854 enforced compulsory religious instruction and asserted strict controls over the elementary teachers. However, the deeper imperatives of commerce and industry were recognized in the government's formal reorganization of the higher elementary schools (known in German countries as 'real schools') into two types, with and without Latin, the latter being very definitely oriented to science, technology and commerce. It was under the provision for those schools that girls' post-primary education began to develop. Many of the lesser German states followed Prussian practices, and this process accelerated with German unification in 1870. State inspection of schools was made universal throughout the empire in 1871, and in 1872 the Falk ordinances, privileging efficiency and useful knowledge over religion, replaced those of Stiehl. German teachers began to organize themselves, establishing incomes and status which their colleagues in other countries scarcely yet enjoyed. German education had been in the van at the beginning of our period, and it was continuing to develop vigorously at the end. In 1900 it was decreed that higher secondary schools (as well as the traditional grammar schools) could lead to university. By 1911, throughout all types of secondary education, about half were providing 'modern' studies.

Russia and Russian Poland

(It should be noted that at this time parts of the former Kingdom of Poland had been absorbed by Prussia and Austria.)

In 1802 Alexander I appointed Russia's first Minister of Public Education, and established a pyramidal system of six universities, controlling one grammar school in each province, district schools (higher elementary and secondary), and parish schools (elementary), the system being confirmed in the 1828 Statute of Primary and Secondary schools, which also laid down that grammar schools and higher education were open only to the nobility. However, reality was very far from matching legislation, and the system came close to working only in the Polish provinces: in 1830, 30.2 per cent of a combined total of 62,672 elementary and secondary pupils were in Poland. From 1833 all education was to be governed rigorously by the three principles of 'orthodoxy, autocracy, nation'. It is not surprising that out of 65 to 70 million inhabitants in 1859 scarcely five million could read. Whether or not Anderson (p.106) overstates the significance of the emancipation of the serfs (beginning in 1861), undoubtedly it did have repercussions for education, though more with respect to proposals for reform than their actual implementation.

Together the legislation of 1864 relating both to elementary schools and grammar schools is very important: all schools – state, church, and private – were declared open to all classes: their function was stated as, 'to strengthen religious and moral notions and spread basic useful knowledge'. Responsibility was shifted to the provinces and the zemstvos, the tight pyramidal structure completely ruptured (Russia, one could say, was the most autocratic of states, but the most ineffectual in maintaining centralized control). The one innovation (very central to one of our concerns), was the creation of 'modern grammar schools' (limited, however, to a quarter of the total), teaching neither Latin nor Greek (and not leading to university). The best work was done by voluntary societies organized by liberal intellectuals, but at the end of the century almost 80 per cent of the population were still illiterate.

At this stage the state was deliberately encouraging schools run by the Russian Orthodox Church, while harassing the schools run by the zemstvos; after 1905 this 'policy' was exactly reversed, but with the schools subject to suffocating censorship and control. Russia remained, what it had been at the beginning of our period, the worst educated of the major powers. Rather late in the day, during the brief experiment with parliamentary government, a law was passed (May 1908), envisaging universal compulsory elementary education within ten years; fevered efforts were made, though the law was actually vetoed by the Czarist autocracy. Poland, as hinted above, had shown the potential for educational progress, but, after 1862, in keeping with points already made about aggressive states and linguistic nationalism, the rule that all education must be conducted in Russian was brutally enforced.

Italy

The Restoration

The restored regimes after 1815 came down with destructive force on whatever rudimentary educational systems already existed. Reaction began in the Kingdom of Naples in 1821, when a Permanent Educational Commission was established, supported by four commissions of investigation, which bore down particularly heavily on elementary education. Large numbers of teachers were sacked, teaching methods censored, pupils in secondary schools put under close surveillance, the English monitorial system, which reformers had been introducing, suppressed as tending to encourage a dangerous independence of spirit (see Ravaglioli, 1982, p.178).

Independence and national unity

Even after unification, Italy remained very much two countries: North and South. The literacy figures we looked at earlier disguised the massive discrepancies between the two parts (in 1860 literacy was almost non-existent in the South, standing at 32% in the North – the overall improvement to 62% by 1890 is a tribute to the educational reform that did take place, though again it was largely in the North). Victor Emmanuel II's Piedmont, in 1859, enacted the Casati Law, a very modest measure calling for two years' compulsory elementary education. This became the basic law for unified Italy but never came near to implementation in the South.

After 1870, the system, in theory, offered the possibilities of:

1   four years of elementary education; prolonged
2   by three years of technical school;
3   secondary education, in
    (a)   a technical institute (continuation of the technical school) for five years, or in
    (b)   a grammar school or college for three years, or
    (c)   (for those training to be primary teachers), in a normal school for three years;

4   university education, divided into five faculties, theology, law, medicine, philosophy and letters, and science and mathematics. In theory all routes to university were open; in practice, as we saw from the statistics, as late as 1900, only 57 per cent of fourteen-to-sixteen-year olds, were in elementary school (with, in fact, even for them, little hope of further progression). At best, the system did no more than train workers and peasants for manual jobs, reserving the best prospects for the upper middle class and nobility.

Ravaglioli (1982, pp.184–6), makes much of the claim that the largely state-sponsored system (in collaboration with the Church) was, in theory, not class-based, but, in my view, pays scant attention to the realities of a very class-divided society, affected throughout by intense poverty.

Britain

In Britain industrialization came first and spread furthest. The nation was cohesive and the state efficient. Anti-state sentiment was stronger than in any of the other major countries.

Scotland, under the influence of the Presbyterian church, had (in its lowland regions) a fairly efficient system of elementary and secondary schools (and it had four prestigious universities). In England, for much of the century, all levels of education remained in the hands of various religious, commercial and voluntary bodies. At the beginning of the century two rival organizations were founded to promote elementary education, the National Society (of the Anglican church) and the British and Foreign Society (of the Nonconformist churches). In the 1830s the government, instead of promoting education directly, began paying subsidies to these two organizations. In 1861 a government commission (the Newcastle Commission) conducted an investigation into the effectiveness of this system: individual members of the commission (including Commissioner Cumin) conducted detailed investigations, and the Commission as a whole sifted the evidence very thoroughly.

Exercise   Read Document III.1, then answer these questions:

1   How reliable is this document for telling us about attitudes to elementary education in mid-Victorian Britain? Does it have any weaknesses?

2   What does the document tell us about working-class attitudes to elementary education, and 'consumer demand'?

Specimen Answers   1   This is the report of a thorough investigation in which schoolmasters, clergymen, ministers, and city missionaries were interviewed. It was in the government's interest (from the point of view of deciding further action) that the report should be as comprehensive and unbiased as possible (as the end of the first extract shows, the government wanted to know how parents would react to any extended educational provision). So, the report should be very reliable. What is missing, however, is direct testimony from members of the working class themselves.

2   It seems the working class do want education for their children – i.e. there is consumer demand. (It is worth noting here that working-class sources, principally working-class autobiographies, confirm this.) But rather than education that aims to be morally uplifting, they want education which will have practical value for their children in teaching 'good reading, writing and arithmetic'.

Nothing was done till 1870; in Britain as well as France, the Prussian victory over France in that year was widely seen as a triumph of the Prussian educational system. The Liberal government, clearly motivated by fears of international economic competition, and by the belief that the new electorate created in 1868 must be given basic education, yet still hesitant about state intervention, gave the two religious organizations a year in which to improve their provision. But at the end of the year there were still large parts of the country with no effective schools; so Forster's Education Act of 1870 created new elementary schools in these areas, to be run by specially elected school boards. In 1881 (Liberal government) elementary schooling was made compulsory, then, in 1891 (Conservative government) free. State secondary schools were not introduced till 1902 (Conservative government).

After the founding of Durham University and two London colleges in the early part of the century, the monopoly of Oxford and Cambridge was only completely broken with the emergence of the civic universities in the second half of the century (very much responses to the needs of commerce and industry, and for an expanded professional class). At its higher levels, and in its élite schools British education, in contrast with continental, remained very free of government supervision.

Here now is a final document exercise (referring back to France, in fact).

Exercise   Turn to Document III.2 and read it carefully.

1   Discuss its nature as a primary source and its strengths and weaknesses as a source for 'Educational Reform in the Early Years of the Third Republic'.

2   Discuss what it tells us (and what it does not tell us) about 'Educational Reform in the Early Years of the Third Republic'.

Note: No historian attempts to interpret a source without having specialist and contextual knowledge. You already have some. But you need to know that the Chamber of Deputies was arranged in a semi-circle with the most radical politicians to the left, the most conservative to the right.

Specimen Answers   1   This is an extract from the official report of proceedings in the French Chamber of Deputies, recording part of the speech of 20 December 1880 by Jules Ferry (the Minister responsible for the burst of educational reform in the early years of the Third Republic), in support of the proposed new law making elementary education compulsory. Its strength is that we have the views of the responsible minister from, as it were, 'the horse's mouth', and, also, some indication of the division of opinion in the chamber. The principal weakness is that the document deals with only one aspect of educational reform, that of compulsory education, and then only with the argument that the basis of this compulsion is moral. To be sure, furthermore, that Ferry's argument is sound, we would need to do what he invites his opponents to do, read the terms of the law itself. There are other comments that could be made (relating, for instance, to how we define 'Early Years'), and congratulations if you made them; however, I think my answer gets to the essence of the way in which all primary sources inherently contain both strengths and weaknesses.

2   No historian ever comes to a primary source without a considerable amount of prior knowledge. From what you already know, you should realize that Ferry is talking about the proposal to make education for six-to-thirteen-year-olds compulsory, which became law in 1881. The obligation, he makes clear, will fall on the father of the family; and the most important thing the document tells us is that Ferry has faith that fathers will accept that this is a moral obligation requiring no further sanctions, though these are there in reserve. By

implication (the 'unwitting testimony', if you like), then, <u>Ferry is tak-ing it for granted that the public now accept</u> (for the various reasons we have encountered throughout our discussion), <u>that compulsory primary education is a national and social necessity;</u> and, anyway, we know from Furet and Ozouf that consumer demand had already had considerable effect *in advance* of the actual legislation. The document gives us a clear perception of where France has arrived at in the debates over education; <u>left and centre support what Ferry is saying</u> – <u>the right continue to oppose compulsory education</u> (which, of course, as we also already know, <u>will be secular</u>, and indeed, <u>republi-can, education</u>). The document also places current developments in the context of past history, confirming the significance of Guizot's Law of 1833 (and also revealing the complications of getting it enforced). The document does not really tell us anything about the detailed motives for educational reform (though we already know them); does not tell us if the Law was actually successful (though we do know that it was passed). Nor, of course, do we learn about the motives of the opposition (though again, as I have suggested, we know, or can guess, them). If the extract only presents the view of one man, he is a rather important one, representative of a wide spectrum of republican opinion. Any single extract will always be limited in what it tells us (historians derive their interpretations from a wide range of documents), but this, as these things go, is quite a rich document.

Language: Instrument of power and of liberation

Exercise 1   How many languages were there in nineteenth-century Europe? Actu-ally I'd be hard put to answer myself. So, as so often in historical study, it's more important that you should show that you understand the nature of the problem, than give a mathematically exact answer (though, of course, in some situations, statistical precision is a basic requirement). Mention some of the less obvious languages. See if you can distinguish between languages with 'family' resemblances and completely distinct languages. Can you think of any 'manufactured' languages? (Anderson mentions at least one.)

2   With regard to language, which was the easier task, unification of Italy or unification of Germany? Explain your answer.

Specimen Answers 1   If you think of all the languages within even the European part of the Russian Empire, and then of Flemish, Occidan (the language of Lan-guedoc in south-west France), Catalan, Alsatian (similar to Swiss German), Sicilian, Neopolitan, Croat, Albanian, and so on, you can get to fifty pretty quickly. The Slav languages form the biggest and most close-knit family, so that a Czech would probably be able to converse with Poles, Russians and Serbs. Hungarian, however, is an utterly different language, with affinities with Finnish; so is Romanian, whose origins are Latin. With regard to 'manufactured' languages, Anderson (p.215) specifically identifies Basque (and makes some cutting remarks about other languages). In a key article, the Cambridge historian Jonathan Steinberg (1987), gives the example of the language created by the Slovak nationalist and poet, Ludovit Stur:

Stur's Slovak was essentially a modern Protestant form of old Czech, the legacy of Jan Hus. It was not at first accepted by Catholics, for whom the old Czech did not belong to their religious heritage ...

... Stur's choice of an artificially homogenised central Slovakian variant forced those Slovaks who had learned to write Czech or those Czechs who regarded the Czechs and Slovaks as one people to make hard choices. In effect, choice of language determined identity, not the other way round. (Steinberg, 1987, p.204)

2   Germany. Educated and uneducated broadly spoke the same language (and education was more widespread). Those who spoke literary Italian were a small minority, and whether one speaks of 'dialects' or 'languages' the overwhelming majority spoke something other than literary Italian. The divide between South (where the language was Neapolitan) and North was very sharp, and that between Piedmont (where the educated favoured French) and the rest of North and Central Italy was quite sharp.

Before I look at the problem of Italy (and then at the less well-known French ones) it is important to clarify some obvious points. Poor communications and lack of national education make for a multiplicity of tongues. Right into the nineteenth century many officials and intellectuals considered Latin (or even Greek) the correct language of scholarship and education. It was in the eighteenth century that the emergence of the vernacular languages (i.e. the languages actually spoken) reached a climax. But while there was a rough agreement about how to speak and write Latin, there was no agreement over Italian. Because of its literary prestige (this for once is not a matter of politics), Tuscan was recognized as the formal language of united Italy – though no one actually, even in Tuscany, spoke literary Tuscan, which, in practical terms, was simply the high-flown language of bureaucrats, lawyers and poets. And in 1861 only two to three per cent of the entire Italian population would have understood this language. It is said that when the Visconti Venosta brothers spoke Italian on the streets of Naples in that very year, they were assumed to be Englishmen!

France had already long been a unified country, and we do have to be clear that the situation there was very different from that of Italy. Still, in 1863, French was not spoken in 8,318 French communes out of a total of

37,510; when compulsory elementary education was instituted, ten per cent of the children turning up for school could speak no French. It was a primary task of both the French and Italian educational systems to inculcate the national language (as Weber, 1976, points out, improved transport and military service also played a part).

In a rather careless cliché, arising from the philosophy of the French post-structuralists of the 1960s, it is sometimes said that language is power. Nothing of the sort. Language is a tool which may deliberately be used as an instrument of power, as when Russian or German governments suppressed Polish, or French ones Occidan, Catalan and Breton. But the tool could be used the other way round. Suppressed nationalities found strength and unity in developing their own special languages. Minority languages could be used as a means of secretiveness from, and defence against, major powers. Catalan was the mother tongue on both the Southern and Northern slopes of the Pyrenees. Peter Sahlins has written:

> ... as the French language was linked to the world of authority and the power of the central state, the use of Catalan could serve members of local society as a means to state their opposition to the state – whether French or Spanish, or both. (Sahlins, 1989, p.264)

Summing up, he writes: 'The Catalan language, then, could and did serve local society as a language of resistance to the state.' The same was true of many other minority languages, whether 'manufactured' ones, like Basque, at the other, Eastern, end of the Pyrenees, and Slovak, or authentic ones, like Czech or Polish.

After 1870 Prussian state officials sought to use the elementary schools in the Polish-speaking areas of East Prussia 'as an instrument of Germanization'. But the officials underestimated 'the difficulties, if not the impossibility, of teaching Polish children to speak and read German in the most impoverished and destitute school system in the Prussian state'. The Poles' own language, you could say, was their secret weapon. In the 1890s the forceful Germanization campaign contributed significantly to the upsurge of Polish nationalism (Lamberti, 1989, p.109).

Conclusion

We live today in a world of nation-states, themselves very much products of developments in the nineteenth century. Yet for thirty years or more now, historians have been increasingly emphasizing forces developing within societies rather than decisions imposed by states. Colleagues have already been discussing the relative significance of Napoleon and of 'the demographic problem'. In concluding my little piece of teaching material, I'd like to make the case that we should give more attention to the rise and spread of literacy as a vital precondition for many other more spectacular developments. Only when we can write our ideas down, can we clarify and refine them (Marwick, 1995). Personally, I'm uncomfortable with phrases such as 'imagined communities of national identity' – decide for yourself on that one. For myself, I don't think there is anything 'imagined' about nationalism (again, look at the world today!). I'd say that prior to the nineteenth century, feelings of nationalism existed, but were unspecific, latent, and overlaid by other, usually imposed, loyalties. Once they could be written about, analysed, and, above all, widely read about, they took on a new specificity and a new force, and could be mobilized politically. Literacy, of course, is, in part, linked to schooling, and schooling is, in part, linked to the growth both of the state and of the economy. But do keep in mind that much of the impulse towards the acquisition of literacy comes from within the family, and is as much a response to social pressures, as to the exigencies of the state.

References

Cauvin, M. (1982), 'L'éducation dans les pays de langue germanique', in G. Mialaret and J. Vial (eds), *Histoire Mondiale de l'éducation*, vol.3, Presses Universitaires de France, Paris, pp.143–161.

Furet, F. and Ozouf, J.(1982), *Reading and Writing: Literacy in France from Calvin to Jules Ferry*, Cambridge University Press, Cambridge.

Gay, P. and Webb, R.K. (1973), *Modern Europe to 1815*, Harper and Row, New York.

Gontard, M. (1982), 'Les Enseignements primaire et secondaire en France' in G. Mialaret and J. Vial (eds), *Histoire Mondiale de l'éducation*, vol.3, Presses Universitaires de France, Paris, pp.251–290.

Hearder, H. (1994),'Whose Identity? Italy and the Italians', in *History Today*, vol.44 (11), pp.37–43.

Lamberti, M. (1989), *State, Society, and the Elementary School in Imperial Germany*, Oxford University Press, New York.

Marwick, A (1995), 'Two Approaches to Historical Study: the Metaphysical (including postmodernism) and the Historical', in *Journal of Contemporary History*, vol.30, no.1, January, pp.5–34.

Maynes, M. J. (1985), *Schooling in Western Europe: A Social History*, Albany, N.Y.

Ravaglioli, F. (1982), 'L'Education dans la peninsule italienne', in G. Mialaret and J. Vial (eds), *Histoire Mondiale de l'éducation*, vol.3, Presses Universitaires de France, Paris, pp.177–96.

Sahlins, P. (1989), *Boundaries: The Making of France and Spain in the Pyrenees*, University of California Press, Berkeley.

Steinberg, J. (1987), 'The historian and the Questione della Lingua', in P. Burke, and R. Porter, (eds), *The Social History of Language*, Cambridge University Press, Cambridge, pp.198–208.

Vincent, D. (1989), *Literacy and Popular Culture, England 1750–1914*, Cambridge University Press, Cambridge.

Weber, E. (1976), *Peasants into Frenchmen: The Modernization of Rural France, 1870–1914*, Stanford University Press, Stanford, Calif.

Unit 14
Culture and Religion

Prepared for the course team by Tony Aldgate and John Wolffe

Contents

Study timetable

Weeks of Study	Text	Video	AC
2.5	Unit 14; Anderson; Offprints 7–10; Documents III.4–7	Video 3	AC2

This unit is divided into two parts: the first deals with Culture during our period and the second with Religion.

Objectives
The objectives of this unit are to enable you to:

1   be aware of the evolution of the press in European cultural history with regard to its changing function as representative of public opinion, with brief reference also to the printed image;

2   become familiar with the broad movements in the arts, in particular 'romanticism' and 'realism' in literature, and 'nationalism' in music;

3   assess the relative significance of 'local' and 'national' cultures by the end of the century, and the characteristics of 'mass culture';

4   appreciate the considerable importance of religious influences in the development of nineteenth-century Europe;

5   appreciate the diversity and complexity of European religion.

Part One: Culture

TONY ALDGATE

Introduction

Historians generally begin with a caution when writing upon the topic of nineteenth-century European culture. And with good reason. Anderson warns of the dangers, you'll note, and says that given the sheer complexity of the subject any attempt 'to summarize it is therefore to falsify, perhaps even seriously to falsify' (p.331). Robert Gildea contemplates the task in lyrical fashion and likens his role to that of 'a solitary figure on the sea-shore'. 'Here and there rises solid rock, the massive and imposing memorials of a Goethe or a Beethoven', he continues, 'but around them lie sheets of pebbles and sandbanks, formless and shifting, representing obscure artefacts, tales without authors, indeed the whole mental activity of mankind'. 'Where to start?' Gildea asks: 'With the brilliant or mundane? With the conscious or the unconscious? With the culture of the social élite or the culture of the masses?' (Gildea, 1991, p.104).

It is, indeed, a vast subject and is generally understood in two key senses: 'the whole way of life' in a society and 'the works and practices' of intellectual, especially artistic, activity in that society. Some aspects have been broached on both fronts, so far, by Bill Purdue and Arthur Marwick in Units 12 and 13 respectively. Marwick examined the many ways in which the growth of literacy and the provision of education impacted upon culture in the widest sense (i.e. fostering 'cultural nationalism', bridging 'cosmopolitan and local popular culture'), and, more specifically, in creating 'demand for certain cultural artefacts, institutions and practices' (e.g. novels, symphony concerts, art galleries). Purdue raised culture in the context of debates surrounding nationalism, not least with his discussion on 'imagined communities', where he explored to what extent it bore the fruits of relatively long-term development and how far it was a new phenomenon related, largely, to nineteenth-century factors (buttressing, for instance, the growth of the nation-state).

The press

I want you to begin by reading what Anderson has to say on the role of the newspaper press in Europe during the nineteenth century. In fact, he really only takes his account up to 1870, in the main, and it is much given to broad brush strokes and overview with little detailed analysis. But it is a useful springboard that allows me to pinpoint key features we shall be following up here and elsewhere.

Exercise   Read Anderson, pp.77–80, 105–6, and 215–17.

1   Generally speaking, what was the role of the press in nineteenth-century Europe?

2   What does Anderson identify as the principal factors affecting its emergence during that time?

3   What kind of press was emerging towards the end of the century and what was its most notable characteristic?

Specimen Answers   1   The role of the press varied from country to country, of course, but – put broadly – it was the 'product of developing social communications' and it served to provide 'a gradual increase in the amount of political information available to the ordinary man', as well as accounting for 'the slow emergence in some parts of the continent of a significant public opinion on political issues' (p.77). The story of the nineteenth-century European press is, in short, the story of the press evolving into what is most commonly identified as the 'Fourth Estate', with all its associated ideals and aspirations, that is freedom of expression and the right to know. That said, Anderson's repeated use of phrases such as 'developing social communications', 'gradual increase' and 'slow emergence', must have alerted you to the fact that the evolution of the press was a fitful process, not easily achieved, and invariably affected by numerous factors.

2   Censorship was one of them. Governments sought to control the press by regulation, outright suppression, or through bribery, because it was viewed with suspicion as a likely source of dissenting or even revolutionary opinion. 'The growth of such powerful engines of information, or misinformation', as Anderson states, 'inevitably had large political implications' though, to repeat, they differed from one country to the next. But, quite simply, 'well before the middle of the century it had begun to be argued that a flourishing newspaper press was an essential sign of a free and flourishing society' (p.78).

The process of industrialization also had its effects in that newspapers could be printed more rapidly and cheaply than ever before, whereas the advent of national news agencies, such as Havas in Paris in 1832, allowed for speedier and widespread dissemination of information to the reading public on a hitherto unheard-of scale. The development of lithography had considerable implications for 'the growth of illustrated periodicals' (p.105) and the introduction of illustrations into newspapers generally.

While these technical innovations were steadily increasing the appeal of the press and it was able therefore both to represent 'popular feeling' and 'exert some influence on the policies of states', as Anderson argues, 'perhaps the best and most obvious index of the fear which the press aroused on the part of governments is their continuing refusal to grant it complete freedom' (p.105).

3   A mass press emerged towards the end of the century. Although it helped to foster the growth of 'new national cultures ... based on mass access to the printed press and the ideas it conveyed', this was largely achieved at the expense of 'local and traditional' cultures. These 'national cultures', like the mass press, were 'increasingly homogeneous' in character (p.215).

Anderson's overview is persuasive and his arguments compelling. But some aspects require scrutiny and others beg questions. Moreover, certain comments, no matter how well informed, are inevitably succinct and need to be carefully elaborated. While Anderson is right, for instance, to mention that 'the press was undeniably important' and politicians sought to cultivate 'good relations with editors and newspapers', his statement that 'no British government during this period was brought down by a press campaign' (p.79), masks much about the turbulent nature of relations between the press and the state. The same can be said for other major European countries as we shall now see in more detail.

Press freedom, public opinion and the state

Read Offprint 7, paying particular attention to the final pages which comprise the section on England. I shall come back to the sections on France and Germany shortly.

Exercise Having read the relevant pages of Offprint 7, I now want you to answer the following questions.

1   How many kinds of newspaper press does Lenore O'Boyle maintain there were in England between 1815 and 1848? What were they, and what realms of public opinion did they represent?

2   Does she see them as being politically significant or powerful?

Specimen Answers 1   O'Boyle suggests that the press in this period could be broadly divided into two categories. First, there was the stamped or 'respectable' press, typified by *The Times*, which served the emergent middle class with news and information relevant to the conduct of business or politics. Second, there was the unstamped or 'radical' press, which was essentially political in character, devoted to airing social grievances, and was for the most part written by and for the working class. The respectable press prospered on the basis of sales and advertising revenue, particularly after the stamp tax on newspapers was reduced by the government. (Though not actually mentioned by O'Boyle, this reduction took place in June 1836 but was accompanied by much stricter powers of regulation and enforcement to ensure that no newspaper could escape the stamp duty which remained.) Thereafter, commercialization made the respectable press wealthy in its own right and it was thereby able to sever those strings which had previously bound it to the government purse. By contrast, the unstamped, radical press was a short-lived phenomenon which, O'Boyle suggests, eventually disappeared because 'many of the evils' associated with industrialization themselves disappeared. (Some commentators would contest this argument, as we shall shortly see, and believe the unstamped press was forced out of existence by those 'very features of the capitalist system' which O'Boyle considers so transitory.)

2   Both sorts of press are invested by O'Boyle with a capacity for political agitation. The respectable press, for example, participated in the cause of parliamentary reform and championed the call for freedom of the press. But the political compromise between the middle class

and the aristocracy, which was achieved with the passage of the 1832 Reform Bill, greatly assuaged the demand for reform. Similarly, the reduction in stamp duty helped to alleviate the demand for freedom of the press, at least for a short while. (This was actually to revive in the 1840s, leading finally to the repeal of the stamp duty in 1855 and the abolition of all the so-called 'taxes on knowledge'.)

Governments could not afford to ignore the respectable press and, as O'Boyle puts it, 'The support of *The Times* was important for any ministry'. (You may also recall, Anderson's comment, p.79, that 'Statesmen such as Canning, Brougham and Palmerston attached great importance to good relations with editors and newspapers'.) But such forms of agitation as were employed by these newspapers 'rested on consensus as to what constituted legitimate government, and on agreement as to the way in which power was to be transferred from ministers who had lost public confidence to an alternative group of leaders'. That one sentence perhaps best summarizes why O'Boyle believes that the respectable press did not actually threaten the political and social order. It might have wished to alter certain features but always within accepted bounds, and its potential for agitation was invariably channelled along constitutional lines. Moreover, the development of the press as an industry and the ever-increasing professionalization of the journalist, made journalism a worthwhile career in itself. That said, O'Boyle distinguishes between English journalists who rarely used the profession as a springboard to politics unlike many of their European counterparts that did. What they got was respectability, she states, what they lacked was the prestige afforded journalists such as Adolph Thiers in their native countries (a point made by Anderson, p.80, who also cites Thiers along with Kossuth and Cavour as further examples). And she quotes John Stuart Mill's cryptic comment to exemplify the view of the English journalist most commonly held by contemporary cultural commentators: 'In France the best thinkers and writers of the nation, write in the journals and direct public opinion; but our daily and weekly writers are the lowest hacks of literature'. Some things, it seems, hardly change. The radical press was, by complete contrast, 'a weapon of war', and a weapon of class war at that. It not only represented the interests of the working class as a 'means of protest and organization' but also posed 'an acutely felt threat' to the classes above it. As O'Boyle implies in her comparison with German journalists, the radical journalists wanted to do more than just 'liberalize society and government'. They saw themselves in the main as 'revolutionaries', committed to the cause of working people, and 'involved in the struggle in the most direct way'.

From the above reading we can see that the radical press existed, then, as a revolutionary and oppositional force throughout the period from 1815 to 1848. Furthermore, as O'Boyle notes, it was a popular press and achieved a larger circulation than the respectable press in that time. The 1850s witnessed the end of all fiscal controls over the press: the Advertisements Duties were abolished in 1853, the Newspaper Stamp Duty in 1855, and the Paper Duties in 1861. Freedom from taxes was assured. Yet, ironically, the radical press virtually disappeared thereafter. What accounts for the loss of this alternative, oppositional voice? Lenore O'Boyle, as we've noted, advances the argument that there was simply no need for it. It was the conditions of early industrialization, she states, that brought the radical press into existence and as the early evils of rapid industialization proved to be transient features, so the radical press proved only a temporary feature of working-class politics. Though Anderson does not even mention the radical press, as such, it is clear from his emphasis on the salutary features of press history in this period that he sees the press emerging as an independent force, suitably equipped to fulfil the ideal of the Fourth Estate as an indispensable link between the people and the governing institutions of the country. (You may have noticed his reference to 'the absence of any censorship' and 'the limited effectiveness of government efforts to influence newspapers', p.77, which perhaps paints too rosy a picture and is certainly debatable, as I am sure you will agree from your reading of O'Boyle thus far.)

As I have hinted already, however, other historians of the press would dispute this line of thought. James Curran (1977), for instance, agues that the traditional variety of controls exercised over the press in the first half of the nineteenth century (legal and fiscal controls) simply did not work. But economic factors and market forces brought about by the industrialization of the press succeeded where other controls had failed in stifling the voice of the radical press. They resulted, quite simply, in the ownership and control of the means of press production being placed beyond the reach of radical publishers with evident implications for the kind of press that obtained thereafter.

Essentially what happened was that developments in the printing press made it possible to produce more papers, but the introduction and maintenance of these machines made the capital required for newspapers much greater than at the beginning of the century. The small owner-editors, relying on letters and news reports from readers, on snippets from other papers, on the piece-work labour of print workers and on the unemployed as street sellers, could no longer compete.

Whereas £15 might have bought a press and £690 launched a paper soon after the turn of the century, by its end it cost closer to half a million pounds for Northcliffe to establish the *Daily Mail*. Circulations might soar but that only increased the scale of production. Just look now at the machine in Figure 1 to get some sense of the scale of technology involved. Moreover, if running costs increased yet the price of a newspaper remained low to stay competitive, then, as you would expect, papers became more and more dependent upon advertising for survival. Advertising was one thing, of course, that the radical press could not count on for revenue. They were, quite simply, aiming at the wrong end of the market and their readers offered little in the way of purchasing power. As one London advertising agent put it succinctly in 1859: 'their readers are not purchasers'. The alternatives presented to the radical press in such circumstances were plain: closure, often with circulations that were large but not enough to sustain a paper; increasing the price per copy and pricing the paper out

Figure 1
Hoe ten-feeder news
machine. (St Bride
Printing Library.)

of the market; or toning down the radicalism and aiming higher up the market in the hope of attracting a different readership, more affluent, and hence also thereby proving more attractive to advertisers. It may be, as O'Boyle argues, that the loss of militancy in the working-class movement accounts for the radical press turning out to be only 'a temporary feature'. But there is enough reason to suggest that Curran has a valid point in arguing that press industrialization was a further, crucial factor in the eclipse of radical journalism.

An additional point is worth bringing in here: what did people want to read? Alongside the radical, unstamped press of the first half of the nineteenth century, and often closely intertwined with it, were popular newspapers focusing on crime and sensation like *The Calendar of Horrors! A Weekly Register of the Terrific, Wonderful, Instructive, Legendary, Extraordinary and Fictitious* which ran in 1835–6. The popular press of the second half of the century latched on to this entertainment aspect and carried a substantial amount of crime and sport.

The continental press and the state

Exercise   Read Offprint 7 once more paying particular attention this time to the sections on France and Germany between 1815 and 1848.

1   What does O'Boyle consider to be the major differences between the role of the mainstream press in (a) France and (b) Germany, compared with its role in England throughout these years?

2   What does she put forward as the main reasons for these various roles?

3   How significant was the press in these countries?

Specimen Answers   1   (a) O'Boyle argues that the press was more politically partisan in France after 1815 and more likely to play an active role in politics than it was in England during this period. Journalists would more readily contemplate a newspaper career as a prelude to political office and, in fact, use one to gain entry to the other.

(b) With regard to Germany, O'Boyle considers that the press was so weak, in comparison with both England and France, that its role was severely limited. There was a certain amount of latitude for the press to express opinions but censorship kept it within strict confines.

2   Political and economic reasons, once again, account for the differing roles played by the press in these three countries. England was the most industrially advanced of the three and could increasingly support a commercial press. After 1832 it was also probably the most politically stable of the three. France, by contrast, did not industrialize much in this time and journalism did not offer a worthwhile career in itself. The press remained dependent upon political patronage and papers were often party political organs. An absorption with political matters contributed to the extreme political orientation of the press. Germany was equally as unindustrialized, if not more so. Political absolutism required control, censorship, and direct regulation because it was believed that papers might provide the means whereby political parties and causes would emerge.

3   Clearly the press in France had a large part to play in political agitation and generating change. As O'Boyle mentions briefly, the press had a part to play in the overthrow of Charles X (a matter also touched upon by Anderson, pp.79–80). In fact the press contributed greatly to the outbreak of revolution in 1830, which began when journalists protested against Charles X's abrogation of press freedom. Printers and publishers barricaded themselves inside their offices in town after town and when surrounded by police and troops, proceeded to fling down revolutionary leaflets to the watching crowds. However, this revolutionary potential should be weighed against the fact, as O'Boyle points out, that newspapers were really weapons used by one fraction of the middle class against another. What was often being sought, as with the respectable press in England, was a change of government 'not mass uprising and a radical overthrow of existing society'.

During this period, the German press did little to upset what O'Boyle describes as the 'condition of equilibrium' which existed or was imposed upon German society. Anderson concurs when stating that in Germany 'only a fairly small minority of the population was effectively reached or influenced by the press' (p.77). It did, however, as both commentators recognize, clearly fulfil an educative function and therefore played a galvanising role in the process of political development.

It should be noted that O'Boyle implies, when talking about Girardin's *Presse* and the *petit journal* type of paper in France, as well as the 'ordinary' or 'sensationalist' press in Germany (broadly equivalent to the 'popular' or 'mass circulation press' in mid-Victorian England), that because they did not deal directly with politics as such and catered essentially for 'amusement' or 'vulgarity' of taste, they were therefore 'apolitical'. This may not be quite so clear cut an argument as first appears. It has been suggested, for instance, that the increasing conformity of the emergent popular press had political implications in itself and contributed substantially to the 'nationalization of culture' which was very much a feature of industrializing societies.

Anderson, you may remember, also cites the mass press which evolved in Europe towards the end of the century as a nationalizing force. It was one agent that 'powerfully fostered the growth of cultures which were not local and traditional, not based on sub-groupings of a relatively small and even intimate kind such as village or regional communities, but increasingly homogeneous over large areas, areas defined by state frontiers' (p.215). This begs many questions, as I have already said, not least about 'local' and 'national' cultures, what we mean by 'homogenization', and so on. Many newspapers at the end of the nineteenth century were local; they were read for their local news, especially at election time. In France, for example, local papers tripled in circulation in the 1870s and increased still more in the 1880s. But they also carried national news, and they existed alongside cheap national papers like *Le Petit Journal*. The 'national' news, especially sensational stories from Paris or overseas, seem particularly and increasingly to have excited the local market. It had been a tradition in peasant France for winter evening meetings (*veillées*) to be held in a barn, stable or sometimes someone's house once or twice a week and for the village story-teller to entertain the assembly; the *veillées* gradually disappeared and the only way to find traditional stories began to be to look for them in books.

Another, and rather different example of the press homogenizing culture can be found in Italy. At the turn of the century the newspapers, beginning with *Giornale d'Italia*, began to provide cultural pages with book and theatre reviews, articles, short stories and novel extracts, consciously setting out to develop a more uniform national taste. It was another way of turning educated Calabrians, Tuscans, Venetians and so on into Italians. Yet it would be wrong to assume that this was an effort made purely from above; the people who read the cultural pages were probably keen to know what was considered culturally important, what were the significant developments in a specifically Italian culture.

We shall be exploring these issues in the section below dealing with 'mass culture' (p.81). For the moment, however, by way of a footnote in further charting the evolution of the press, I want you to look at the following three printed images. The first is a James Gillray cartoon of 10 February 1808; the second, an illustration from an 1859 edition of the Berlin periodical *Kladderadatsch* celebrating the centenary of Schiller's birth (the legend, incidentally, announces 'The only thing and the only one on which Germany is in agreement'); the third is from a British periodical, *The Cottager and Artisan*, for January 1866.

Figure 2
James Gillray cartoon entitled Very Slippy-Weather *and dated 10 February 1808.*
Copyright: British Museum.

Figure 3
Das Einzige und Der Einige worin Deutschland einig ist. From Facsimile
Querschnitt durch den Kladderadatsch. *v.5 (Munchen, Scherz Verlag, 1965)*

Figure 4
Turning over a new leaf from the British periodical, The Cottager and the Artisan, *for January 1866. Photo: The British Library.*

Exercise   Study the background and the publishing details of the Gillray cartoon (Fig. 2) and note how this differentiates the way that it was presented to the public from the two periodical illustrations?

Discussion   The background to the Gillray cartoon shows Humphrey's print shop in St James's Street where the cartoons were published and shown in the window for potential buyers, and anyone else who cared to look. The other illustrations, arguably more sharply or cleanly drawn and presented (easier, of course, given the technical advances in lithography) were incorporated into periodicals.

Figure 5
James Gillray cartoon, entitled Maniac Ravings *and portraying Napoleon as 'Little Boney'. (Mansell Collection.)*

Gillray is best known for his savage political cartoons during the Revolutionary and Napoleonic period. If you were familiar with his work you may notice some of his more famous cartoons sketched in Humphrey's window. As well as ridiculing Britain's politicians, Gillray also ridiculed her enemies (notably 'Little Boney', see Fig. 5) and drew several cartoons with a sympathetic, but much put upon, John Bull. These are all images which you should think about with reference to nationalism and national culture;

how far was it formulated essentially in response to external threats? Remember Bill Purdue's discussion of Linda Colley's work. But the fact that Gillray's work was published and put on show for sale in London makes another point – how many people in Britain can have been familiar with it? The same point might be made for other countries, though there censorship impeded the work of would-be Gillrays. In France in the 1830s Honoré Daumier fell foul of the authorities regularly for his cartoons mocking the monarchy, its government, finance and the law. Daumier's work was commonly exhibited in the Paris printshop of Aubert and in *Tableau de Paris*, published in 1852, Edmond Texier declared that 'one could say, without much exaggeration, that more than one revolution began before Aubert's window' (Texier, 1852, ii, p.164). A good story, but unlikely. However, by the 1830s, technological developments had enabled such cartoons to be circulated in periodicals. Daumier was closely connected with two such, *La Caricature* and, later, *Le Charivari*. The model of these periodicals was rapidly adopted elsewhere, including England where the weekly *Punch. The London Charivari* took this form.

Exercise What cultural messages do the two illustrations (Figs 3 and 4) intend to convey?

Discussion Schiller is clearly being represented as the symbol of highest expression of cultural value and his image used to invoke German national identity. For all the diversity of local communities gathered together, the people are united in venerating his worth. The image espouses, in short, the importance of cultural tradition. By contrast, the British illustration is parochial and naturalistic in its concerns but the image is still clearly intended to represent more than it depicts with an obvious emphasis on home, hearth and family – they are plainly decent, respectable (and well-provisioned) folk with the Bible, noticeably, in use. The values it seeks to inculcate are evident and the image is partial and selective, clearly projecting a preferred vision of everyday life.

Though I don't want to set too much store by a very small selection of images, they do serve to highlight two points. For a start, lithographical developments by the middle of the century afforded greater latitude for a pictorial representation of the world which depended most upon visual characteristics for its impact, without recourse to much by way of word-caption accompaniment, and was therefore, perhaps, also more easily understood. Hence, in part, the profusion of illustrated periodicals by mid-century and their undoubted appeal. (One historian, Patricia Anderson (1994), argues that technical advances transformed the printed image at this time, making it widely accessible, and, in consequence, discerns the beginnings of a 'mass culture' around 1860 rather than later in the century, as most historians would have it.) Second, the imagery represented in these periodicals had a larger purpose than mere diversion or illustration and was principally intent upon fostering belief in an idealized version of national or community culture. It is, in short, being utilized to ideological effect. If one is looking for evidence of the press's capacity to conjure 'imagined communities', one need look no further than the illustrated press, but as with the cultural pages of the Italian press described above, it would be wrong to think solely of these images of the nation and its culture being imposed from above, and that alone.

The arts

Broaching the matter of widespread movements in the arts can be a tricky business and always invites problems of definition. I want you to start by turning to Anderson though, in this instance, I do not intend setting any exercises upon him. I want you to plot his elaboration of 'romanticism' and 'realism' against your reading of the two literary extracts which follow below. Note, for example, the extrapolation of 'subjectivism' and 'stressing of the individual' as fundamental traits of the former, while interest in 'social mechanisms' and indifference to 'the deeper aspects of individual personality' are cited as typical of the latter. What else, helps to define these two movements and the place of literature within them? Anderson has little, if anything, to say about music and nationalism but look, all the same, at what he writes about music generally. So, read those pages in Anderson's chapter 7 covering the arts (pp.331–45, 365–9).

From 'romanticism' to 'realism'

Read Documents III.4 and 5. The former comprises the author's introduction (added for the 3rd edition, 1831), and a short extract (the same in both the 1831 edition and original 1818 text), from Mary Shelley's *Frankenstein*; the latter consists of the author's preface and opening few pages to Giovanni Verga's *I Malavoglia* (*The House by the Medlar Tree*), first published in Italy in 1881.

Exercise 1   What contrasts can you immediately discern in the themes and styles of each?

2   What do they suggest about the concerns of the respective novelists? (I'm not looking for a full-blown critique, incidentally, just instinctive reactions and impressions for the moment.)

Specimen Answers 1   It's obvious, I'm sure, how markedly different they are which is no surprise given Mary Shelley's avowed intent to write 'a ghost story' that would 'awaken thrilling horror ... curdle the blood, and quicken the beatings of the heart', whereas Giovanni Verga aimed to write 'an honest and dispassionate study ... [of] the humblest people in society'. On the face of it, Shelley's piece is a trifling diversion, Verga's has grander (nobler?) ambitions. Moreover, Shelley has chosen a fanciful, even fantastic, theme – no less than the creation of life (albeit resulting in 'a monster'); she seeks to conjure an atmosphere filled with heightened emotion and dread; uses evocative settings; and employs florid language throughout with the occasional literary allusion. The milieu is definitely one of exalted circles (the literati she moves among, and the scientist she writes about); notice, also, the individualist emphasis as a linchpin of the plot and the author's account of its genesis – the repeated use of the subjective 'I' in each instance. Verga's story, by contract, is a story of everyday folk; it

Unit 14: Culture and Religion 79

deals with the ordinary and mundane, is drained of overt emotion, if anything, though strong on characterization, naturalist locations, vernacular speech patterns, and its theme is seemingly fatalistic in suggesting one must accept one's lot as befits the social order and however unfortunate the results. It is objective in intent and distinctly plebeian in tone.

2   Put simply (and crudely), Shelley is hardly concerned with this world while Verga is very much in and of it. Shelley's concerns are lightweight and insubstantial, merely escapist and entertaining, whereas Verga's purpose is credible, even laudable. Shelley, you might go so far as to say is the obvious 'romantic' and Verga the evident 'realist'.

That is a crude judgement, to repeat, and grossly unfair of course. The novels come from different genres, for a start, so I'm not comparing like with like. Shelley's novel is done a grave misjustice in any such reading. Mary Shelley (the daughter of radical parents, Mary Wollstonecraft and William Godwin, and wife of the poet) was only too aware of the time in which she was writing. If her theme was ultimately far-fetched (and chosen anyway, remember, to fulfil the criteria of a horror story), she was well read and well versed in events of the period and it showed, to advantage, in her book. (Also giving rise, incidentally, to now current re-assessments of both book and author which stress her prescience and relevance, not least in feminist history.)

If we were to take the comparison further then we should have to add that it is necessary to take into account the critical and public reception afforded the novels before finally judging their relative merits or respective worth. In this regard, Shelley scores especially well. *Frankenstein* was favourably received on initial publication in 1818, turned into a stage play in the 1820s, and the somewhat amended third edition of 1831 was reprinted many times. *I Malavoglia*, by contrast, proved a disappointment to Verga for its lack of success with critics and the Italian reading public on publication in 1881, and even the publication of a French translation in 1887 did little to amend matters. The critical plaudits it eventually earned as heralding the arrival of Italy's 'first modern novel' were slow in coming.

One can quite see why Anderson quotes, approvingly, Gustave Corbet's dictum that 'Realism is essentially a democratic art' (p.366). Given its new-found depiction of the people, everyday life, the ordinary and the mundane, rendered in a naturalist fashion scarcely evident before, there was much about the 'realist' movement, writers and painters, that was genuinely democratic in theme and spirit. But in the case of Verga, for all his emphasis upon 'realist' intent and representing 'reality as it was', he clearly had little impact with *I Malavoglia*. What price 'realism' if it was merely producing 'art for art's sake'? It's a rhetorical question, of course. There were many 'realist' writers who scored popular success and achieved considerable following as did the French novelist, Emile Zola. My point is a simple one. To do justice to Shelley, Verga and their novels, one must examine not just the texts alone but also the contexts within which they were written and circulating. And despite the corrective rejoinders I've now lodged for myself about some all too crude and casual initial judge-ments (deliberately done, of course, to tease out your own reactions along the way), the exercise has not been without another purpose which should still hold good. If nothing else, I trust it has alerted you to the simple point that there were pronounced sea changes in literary movements as with the arts, generally, between the outset and demise of the nineteenth century. Moreover, the documents were chosen to exemplify stylistic and thematic features traditionally associated with the two key movements – 'romanticism' and 'realism' – though, to repeat, the texts alone (even in their entirety and with a lot more examples besides) are not enough to fill in the picture. It is also essential to have a grasp of their historical contexts of production and reception. Nowhere is this more evident than when broaching the topic of music.

Music and nationalism

'The nationalist impulse of a composer bent on dramatizing his nation, for all his vivid assertion, cannot turn an abstract medium into something that communicates a clear national image', Jan Smaczny comments in his dis-cussion of Czech musical identity during the nineteenth century (on AC2). Smetena's *The Brandenburgers in Bohemia* (1865) drew its inspiration from French, Italian and German sources as much as anything else; although his comic opera *The Bartered Bride* (1866) quoted from folk song and included characteristic popular dances like the polka, it also borrowed heavily from other operatic traditions.

'Music *per se*, even if it includes references to folk song or is mod-elled on it', Trevor Bray agrees, 'is not necessarily nationalist or other-wise'. Weber, after all, adapted a 'German' folk tune for the huntsman's chorus in his comic opera, *Der Freischutz (The Marksman)*, first per-formed in Berlin in 1821 and greeted by its audience as 'a new type of specifically German opera'. Weber was hailed as 'a new national voice'. But the melody he chose was French in origin. Liszt, acclaimed 'a national hero' in Hungary, was a cosmopolitan composer and his style consciously eclectic. He lived there permanently for just 10 years of childhood, did not return until 18 years later, and barely spoke his native language. The rhapsodies he claimed were based in part on native folk music – Hungarian gypsy music – were written by nineteenth-century middle-class dilettantes. In Italy, Verdi was compelled to submit the libretto for his opera *Nabucco* (1842) to censorship scrutiny by the governing authorities to ensure it did not offend Austrian susceptibilities. Little room, it seems, for nationalist sentiment there.

Exercise

You should now listen to AC2 and then list what four factors distinguish nationalist music?

Specimen Answers

1   Intent. Weber and Smetena, for instance, were consciously seeking to create operatic traditions in keeping with burgeoning nationalist sen-timent. If that meant borrowing from other traditions or appropriat-ing 'foreign' musical influences, then so be it, given, especially, that they were reworked to meet new-found nationalist needs and circum-stances.

2   Theme. This inevitably entails drawing upon a nation's history, mythology or landscape as inspiration or storyline for a musical work. It might be done overtly (as with Smetena's symphonic poem *My Country* or Weber's use of German folklore for the libretto of *The Marksman*), or in less explicit if still locally identifiable fashion (as with Verdi's *Nabucco*, for instance, where the plight of the Hebrew captives in Babylon of c.6 BC served as an allegory for the Italian situation and was clearly understood as such in nationalist circles).

3   Style. This meant utilizing melodic styles, folk songs, dances and instruments (e.g. bagpipes used by both Dvorak and Smetena, a Hussite hymn employed by Smetena, *singspiel* for Weber, the *verbunkos* for Liszt) that were either demonstrably local in origin or, once more, perceived as such.

4   Language. This includes Weber's use of his native German as the language for his libretti thereby breaking with tradition and the overwhelming domination of Italian as the customary language for opera.

Despite the highly abstract nature of the medium they are dealing with, Trevor Bray and Jan Smaczny identify much of nationalist import or characteristic in nineteenth-century music. 'Music was a powerful means of fixing or propagandizing a perceived national identity', Smaczny states, not least 'in countries dominated by a stronger power'. Thus, for the Czechs and the Italians 'nationalist' music was inevitably invested with 'political associations'. (Remember, of course, such 'associations' need not always be so welcome. Given its revolutionary connotations, for instance, the 'Marseillaise' was frowned upon by French governments throughout most of the nineteenth century.) To understand the way in which music was perceived, in short, both Bray and Smaczny stress, is necessary to any understanding of 'nationalist' music.

Mass culture

For all the caveats sensibly lodged by Anderson about the difficulties which beset any attempt at surveying European culture by the turn of the twentieth century, some essential features can be discerned. The social and economic conditions essential for the development and dissemination of cultural activities on a vast scale were all there, for instance, at the end of the nineteenth century – the spread of elementary education and enhanced levels of literacy; large and concentrated urban populations; a relative gain in real terms of the incomes of large sections of this urban populace which allowed for the regular, cheap purchase of 'entertainment'; slowly increasing amounts of leisure time available for 'recreation and enjoyment'; the introduction and improvement of urban public transport systems which permitted late night travel, for example, from city centres to residential suburbs; and the application of new-found technologies to many spheres of cultural production, allied to their widespread commercial exploitation. Urbanization and industrialization, in short, had a distinct effect upon the cultural landscape. We have also noted, in passing, mention of a marked <u>tendency towards the 'nationalization' and 'homogeneity' of European cultures</u>, generally. How valid are these terms, however, and what do they mean for the period 1870–1914?

Exercise   Read Offprints 8 and 9 now.

1   List, briefly, the major examples cited by Harris as evidence of a diverse and continuing 'local' culture, and those which <u>militated</u> towards the 'nationalization' of culture in Britain. (Reviewing TV1 would also be helpful.)

2   How then, on balance, does she view British culture?

3   Where does Gildea differ, if at all, in his assessment of European culture?

Specimen Answers   1   The rich and variegated nature of 'local' culture is exemplified by several key features: the 'civic pride of many provincial cities' as shown in the building of town halls, public libraries, hospitals, art galleries and civic universities; the 'preservation of local autonomy and custom' which resisted bureaucratic centralization, enjoyed a tremendous resurgence in the 1840s and 1850s, and meant, for example, that '<u>much of the cultural life of early Victorian Britain flourished, not in the metropolis, but in the provinces and in Scotland</u>'; '<u>local democracy</u>', as manifested in the establishment of schools boards, county councils, parish and district councils, as well as the provision of public utilities such as gas and water. Also, of course, the advent of popular recreations like football and county cricket acted as an obvious <u>spur to</u> what Harris describes (somewhat politely, perhaps, in view of the fierce rivalries football generated pretty much from the outset) as '<u>local patriotism</u>'.

By contrast, <u>innovations like the railways, telegraph, the postal service, the 'retailing revolution' and the arrival of mass circulation newspapers, all served to transform 'perceptions of the boundaries of community and national life</u>'. So, too, did the gradual renaissance of London as 'a centre of fashionable and artistic life', with its vast array of new theatres, galleries and concert halls.

(You should at this point consider also some of the points arising in TV1. 'Napoleon III's interest in developing the infrastructure of his capital', Tim Benton states, 'was matched by his desire to maintain Paris as a "Cultural Mecca" '. Hence, Napoleon III employed the architect Louis Visconti to combine the Tuileries Palace and the Louvre into a massive complex 'celebrating cultural and political power'. To maintain his scheme for 'the cultural supremacy of Paris', furthermore, a competition was held in 1857 to find an architect for a new opera house which would act as 'a focus of France's cultural identity'. Though not completed until 1875, it still served the intended dual function of sumptuous opera house and palatial centre for the social élite as well as for the entertainment of foreign dignitaries in the cause of a new France seeking to re-establish its cultural credentials under the Third Republic. Similarly, <u>the new Italian</u> state wanted to build a specifically Italian cultural monument in the centre of Rome. Whether the Victor Emanuel monument (again see TV1) is a model of Italian culture remains a moot point – it is certainly unique!)

Last, by no means least, an increasing standardization in the English language and the way it was spoken, did a lot both to stigmatize regional dialects or local accents, and engender linguistic conformity. Though nothing new in itself, of course, and very much part of a long, slow socializing process, the notion of language 'as a badge of social status ... acted as a powerful force for restructuring an older, regional, variegated, and customary society along more uniform, national and horizontal lines' (a factor already cited by Arthur Marwick in Unit 13).

2   On balance, Harris plainly views British culture as increasingly homogeneous in character. Though never wishing to underestimate the importance of provincial culture, and despite always acknowledging the different yet still vital traditions which obtained in Scotland, Wales and Ireland (with Dublin singled out by a footnote, you will see, as especially significant in its own right), Harris plainly views British society as manifesting a distinct tendency towards uniform, standardized notions of cultural value and worth. Hence, her choice of phrase, 'nationalization of culture', to describe the trajectory of the British experience which Harris believes was somewhat unlike the continental European one (albeit that she really only mentions a measure of difference in its 'centralizing' import than anything else).

3   Gildea is less inclined to stress the contrasts between British and other European cultures (though he draws interesting comparisons, specifically, about the basis of class appeal for football in Britain, France and Germany), and is set rather upon spotlighting the obvious points of similarity across the various countries. Mind you, he too is acutely aware of the diversity and plurality of 'local' cultures (witness his comments on the German press and French sport), and he is also alert to the strength of the 'nationalizing' impulse in European cultures (see, for example, his remarks upon the working men's choral societies in Germany which, plainly, he feels lost something of their initial impetus as an oppositional class force when they acquired 'artistic pretensions' in keeping with the middle-class 'nationalistic' clubs).

But Gildea is more intent upon extrapolating from European cultural experience across the board. Thus, he mentions the popular press and pulp fiction, music halls, cabaret and variety along with boulevard theatre, seaside resorts, and cinema, as common exemplars of a 'cheap' culture which met with considerable success, while serious cultural fare which sought to arouse 'nobler passions' usually wilted in the face of commercial failure. Gildea's account of sport plays upon the same lines of divide in highlighting the changes which ensured when the traditional amateur code of sport – as expressed in Baron de Coubertin's idealist notion that the revived Olympics should seek to 'unify and purify' – was profoundly affected by the introduction of a professional code.

Professionalism, Gildea agues, was attended by exploitation on a grand scale. This was shown, at its most acute, in British football and

French cycle racing. Betting on the pools and a weekly football news-paper followed fast upon the advent of professionalism to the former; newspaper advertisements taken by cycle manufacturers leading, in turn, to the self-same newspapers sponsoring road races to boost their circulations, followed in the wake of professionalization of the latter.

'The wheel had come full circle, as business, sport, and the popular press all fed off each other', Gildea neatly comments (thereby rein-forcing his argument, you may recall, that 'news as education was replaced by news as entertainment' in the popular press). The hom-ogeneity which Gildea discerns, in short, owed less to any national-ization of cultures and more to an emergent mass culture which inevitably accompanied the processes of urbanization and industrial-ization.

MAY

In one key respect, furthermore, Gildea's account differs from Harris. While also stressing the matter of homogeneity, he introduces a notion of quality. Mass culture was 'trash', 'filth', 'corrupting', it provided 'semi-pornographic' entertainment. These are not his judgements, of course, but the judgements circulating among 'conservative, religious and cultivated circles' and the 'bourgeois and proletarian moralists' who engaged in battle against the 'popular taste' and sought instead to propagate a 'high' culture that would arouse the 'nobler passions' and prove morally uplifting. The musical director of the Deutsche Arbeiter Sangerbund, quoted by Gildea, was not alone in thinking that the proletariat should be encouraged to enjoy, for example, 'the finest fruits from the cornucopia of the goddess of music', which meant Bach, Handel and Beethoven in preference to the popular fare forthcoming at a local music hall, or elsewhere. To such people, mass culture was invariably a debased culture.

Most of these ideas were hardly novel or original. Matthew Arnold's *Culture and Anarchy*, in 1869, had advanced the thesis that culture was 'the pursuit of perfection' and that 'the great men of culture are those who have had a passion for diffusing, for making prevail, for carrying from one end of society to the other, the best knowledge, the best ideas of their time'. And his sentiments had been echoed by many cultural commen-tators. What was new by the end of the nineteenth century, however, was that these culturally élitist opinions were buttressed by the writings of vari-ous European social psychologists who expressed growing fears about the 'herd instinct' and 'suggestibility' of the masses. The Frenchman, Gustave Le Bon, was the leading popularizer and publicist of the 'crowd theorists' with his 1895 book, *The Crowd: A Study of the Popular Mind* (mentioned under its French title by Anderson, p.362), which was translated into thir-teen different languages, reprinted twenty-six times in France and a dozen times in an English edition. Le Bon, along with his fellow Frenchman, Gab-riel Tarde, and the Italian, Scipio Sighele, appeared to lend scientific credibility to notions about the 'corruptibility' of the masses. It certainly fuelled the worst fears of the cultural élites on that score.

What, though, was there to fear in mass culture? Despite the fact that 'news as entertainment' replaced 'news as education' in the pages of the popular press, wherein lay the danger if, as Gildea recounts, daily news-papers were 'scarcely "political" at all'? If, as he repeatedly implies, mass culture was merely the conduit for 'entertainment', what was the harm in that? To explore these questions briefly, in conclusion, let us look at one artefact which, as Gildea rightly states, transformed the realms of popular culture and turned out to be a considerable mass phenomenon: film.

Gildea sketches film's origins and evolution from fairground attraction to full-scale exhibition in purpose-built cinemas. Demand grew as the novelty of early actuality film was supplemented by regular programmes comprising newsreel material and feature films (with attractive stars, exciting stories, engaging themes). For every Louis and Auguste Lumière, intent upon utilizing film to advantage in rendering scenes of everyday people and events, unmanipulated activity of more or less general interest, there was a George Méliès, determined to exploit it to the full by playing with the image, conjuring trick effects, and generally realizing its fantasy value. From pretty much the outset, in short, film's properties as both a 'realist' and 'fictional' medium were employed to great effect.

Figure 6
Cronje's surrender at Paardeberg. South African National Film, Video and Sound Archives, Pretoria.

Figure 7
Attack on British Red Cross tent from an untitled 'fake' film. South African National Film, Video and Sound Archives, Pretoria.

The point is well demonstrated in the three stills found in Figures 6, 7 and 8 which are all from British Boer War film material. Look at Figures 6 and 7, now, and see if you can immediately distinguish the actuality film from recreated footage. The first is genuine, if hardly very exciting or

Figure 8
Set-to between John Bull
and Paul Kruger. South
African National Film,
Video and Sound Archives,
Pretoria.

eventful, which is no surprise really given such limiting factors as the sheer weight of camera equipment available at the time. W.K.L. Dickson's equipment weighed a ton and required a ox cart to ferry it round, thereby severely curtailing his camera movement and field of vision.

Figure 7 is obviously a recreation of the event it claims to depict and a pretty dramatic one, too – what with the nurse (in her clean uniform) being rescued by two soldiers, while the dead or wounded lie nearby and flags waft in the breeze. Figure 8 is of a different provenance altogether. Neither actuality film nor recreated fake, it is a patriotic jingoistic little piece entitled 'Set-to between John Bull and Paul Kruger', full of simplistic allegory and blatant symbolism. Kruger kicks John Bull, waves a white flag when requiring a rest, attacks from behind as necessary, yet still contrives to lose the fight at the last while John Bull emerges triumphant.

Conclusion

On p.76 (above), I noted how, at the beginning of the century, James Gillray's John Bull was a sympathetic but much put upon character; he was, it could be argued, a representation of the English 'common man', generally full of plain, common sense, but burdened by the government's demands for taxes and military manpower. In this Boer War film (and in other representations at the close of the nineteenth century) John Bull stands for a different kind of Englishness. He is open, honest, and would never dream of striking an opponent whose back was turned. This late nineteenth-/early twentieth-century image is probably the one which English people liked to perceive for themselves especially when it came to making comparisons with foreigners. It is propaganda, of course, but it is propaganda that draws on a comfortable and comforting national self-perception.

When we come to look at culture and nationalism we are faced with a chicken and egg problem. John Bull, France's Marianne, the German Michael and so on, intend what propagandists want them to, but if they do not strike a chord with the audience then they are poor propaganda. Other national portrayals in press, cartoon, caricature, and eventually film were similar. And there is a further problem: across Europe at the end of the nineteenth century members of the élite were condemning mass culture for its vulgarity, its focus on sport, violence and lasciviousness. Did this constitute the beginnings of an homogenized western popular culture? Or has it always been there, in violent fairy stories like those, for example, collected in early nineteenth-century Germany by the brothers Grimm and those which padded the repertoires of the storytellers in French village *veillées*, as well as the unstamped press in England? Is this a case, finally, of the élite now hoping to control the culture of the majority with their own notions of what is best for them, and best for the state and society?

Part Two: Religion

JOHN WOLFFE

Introduction

During the Franco-Prussian War of 1870–1, as German armies besieged Paris, and France passed through the darkest hour of her nineteenth-century history, a refugee from the capital conceived the idea of a national vow to build a new church there when the country's fortunes improved. The movement caught on, and the result was the erection of the Sacré-Coeur Basilica on the hill of Montmartre where it remains today one of the most prominent and famous landmarks of Paris. Small donations made up a very substantial proportion of the money raised for the construction of the church, an indication that it reflected genuinely widespread feeling rather than just the obsession of a small wealthy minority. Building began in 1875 and continued for the next four turbulent decades. The church was eventually consecrated in 1919, by which time it had already established itself as a potent symbol of national will and identity in the face of the titanic struggle of the First World War (Benoist, 1992, pp.209–40, 429).

The year after the foundation stone of the Sacré-Coeur was laid, in July 1876, five young German girls were bilberrying in woods near their home village of Marpingen in the Saarland. They were frightened at seeing a mysterious woman in white carrying a child, an apparition which returned several times and was quickly identified by adults as the Blessed Virgin. The village quickly began to attract considerable numbers of pilgrims, a development regarded with mixed feelings by the church authorities who were liable to be uneasy at such expressions of unofficial religion. Meanwhile the Prussian government responded with notable heavy-handedness. It was currently waging a campaign against Catholicism at the national level (the *Kulturkampf* (see Unit 2)) and sent soldiers in to repress these manifestations of popular devotion. Considerable political controversy ensued and the affair was debated at length in the Prussian Parliament in January 1878. Marpingen became a focus for debate over the situation of religion in Germany after the unification of 1871, with Catholicism under attack both from Protestants and from secular liberals.

I have chosen these two incidents to open this part of the unit as they both illustrate how in the second half of the nineteenth century currents of religion, politics, culture and national identity could become very much intertwined. The study of the history of religion in our period raises questions that go far outside the internal history of the churches and spiritual life. How widespread among the population was committed religious belief? How did the religious experience and expectations of the 'ordinary people' relate to the teachings of the churches? What implications did the presence (or absence) of Christian conviction have for social and cultural life? How did it affect the development of European states? How important was people's religious consciousness in shaping their awareness of the national and political units to which they belonged?

In this part of the unit I shall first offer a general survey of the European religious scene stressing its institutional, traditional and geographical diversities. We shall then consider – on the basis of an extract from Hugh Mcleod's *Religion and the People of Western Europe 1789-1970* – some of the structural changes in the place of religion in European societies that took place during our period. The remainder of the space will be taken up with two case studies – one of France, the other of Ireland – which will provide you with more specific illustrations of the issues explored in the earlier pages and also relate religion to the wider development of these two nations.

At the outset, however, it is important to acknowledge one key limitation imposed by space. Although predominantly Christian, nineteenth-century Europe had significant religious minorities. Muslims were to be found in the sphere of Turkish influence in the Balkans. Jews were much more widely dispersed across the continent, relatively substantially more numerous than they are at the present time, after their numbers were depleted in the mid-twentieth century by the Holocaust and by migration to Israel. It is impossible to discuss these groups in detail, but their presence must not be forgotten.

Patterns of European religion

Anyone who travels across Europe, or just from Cork to Belfast, or from Munich to Berlin, can hardly fail to be struck by the diversities of religious adherence between neighbouring countries, and often between different regions of the same country. Colourful and elaborately decorated Catholic and Orthodox church buildings contrast with more austere Protestant ones; wayside shrines and lists of mass times contrast with posters of biblical texts. Such differences are – even at the end of the twentieth century – so much part of the fabric of our environment that we seldom give them much thought. When, however, we consider the extent and significance of religious variation in the nineteenth century, a period in which in most parts of Europe all possible measures of religious observance and identification were much higher than in our own era, we are indeed touching at a mainspring of people's identity and distinctiveness.

To an important extent the religious map of nineteenth-century Europe still reflected the legacy of divisions within Christianity which had originated centuries in the past. The schism between the Eastern and Western Churches, conventionally dated to 1054, left Russia, Greece, and Serbia, and their respective spheres of influence in the east and south-east of the continent, with a tenaciously held sense of their Orthodox identity. Orthodoxy is distinguished from other forms of Christianity by the great importance accorded to liturgical ritual as a medium of conveying religious truth, and by the centrality of icons (pictures regarded as channels of divine grace) in worship. The Orthodox world was by no means monolithic. Churches were organized on a national basis and, although there was no large-scale separation comparable to the Reformation in the West, disputes, notably over liturgy, did lead to schism. Also in Eastern Europe, especially in Ruthenia and the Ukraine, were to be found so-called Uniate churches which were Orthodox in terms of liturgy and theology, but Catholic insofar as they acknowledged the primacy of the Pope.

The conviction of Orthodox nations that they possessed a purer and more authoritative strand of Christian belief does much to explain the vigour with which across the centuries they resisted western culture and political influence. This was strikingly illustrated at the battle of Borodino in September 1812, when the Russians confronted Napoleon's invading army. Before the battle, Kutusov, the Russian commander, paraded around his troops accompanied by clergy in their vestments and the greatly-venerated icon of the Madonna of Smolensk. According to a member of Napoleon's staff:

> This solemn spectacle, the exhortations of the officers, the benedictions of the priests, finally aroused the courage of the spectators to a fanatical heat. Down to the simplest soldier, they believed themselves consecrated by God to the defence of Heaven and the sacred soil of Russia. (Blanning, 1985, p.211)

The sequel was one of the bloodiest battles of all time, during which 40,000 Russians died in the course of inflicting losses of equal magnitude on the French and hence giving a severe check to their prospects of subduing Russia (Blanning, 1985, pp.211–13). As the nineteenth century wore on, the memory of such formative interactions between religious and national consciousness served, notably in the Crimean War of 1854–6, to reinforce European perceptions of the distinctive and somewhat mystical character of Russian identity.

Meanwhile in the sixteenth and seventeenth centuries the Western Church had been bitterly divided by the struggles of the Reformation and Counter-Reformation. It is important for you to appreciate that in terms of the generally received perception of the importance of the Catholic–Protestant divide within Western Christianity; the nineteenth century was much closer in spirit to the seventeenth century than to the twentieth. The distinction still seemed to touch at the heart of what it was to be a Christian. Did authority in religion come from the traditions and hierarchy of an infallible Church, or through individual interpretation of the divinely-inspired Scriptures? Was eternal salvation obtained through a lifetime of constant attendance at the sacraments of the Church or through a single life-changing encounter with God in conversion? Did God need to be mediated to the individual believer by saints and the Church, or could each humble soul come face to face with its maker without such assistance?

True, heretics were no longer burnt at the stake, but Roman Catholic clergy still preached with deadly sincerity their conviction that there was 'no salvation outside the Church' and that even if Protestants could now escape incineration in this world, they were still doomed to the flames of Hell in the next. If anything the Roman Catholic Church's dogmatic stance stiffened in the second half of the nineteenth century, with the rise of Ultramontanism, meaning the centralization of power in the papacy. This trend was manifested in developments such as the Syllabus of Errors (1864), the First Vatican Council with its declaration of papal infallibility (1870) and the papal condemnation of Anglican priestly orders (1896). (It was probably no coincidence that these developments coincided with the collapse of the papacy's temporal authority and the establishment of the kingdom of Italy which heightened the Catholic Church's sense of being politically embattled (see Unit 2). A more dogmatic and authoritarian ecclesiastical structure was regarded as the most effective response to such challenges.) Protestants, for their part, readily equated Rome with deadly religious error, proclaiming that its teaching led human souls away from authentic encounter with God. Moreover, especially at times of political and social crisis, they were prone to interpret their contemporary rivalry with Catholicism in the cataclysmic terms suggested by Revelation, the last book of the Bible. The Pope was liable to be viewed as Antichrist, and Rome linked with Babylon, the mother of abominations, which was to be the central target of divine judgement at the anticipated Second Coming of Christ. Beliefs of this kind were particularly apparent at the time of Revolutions of 1848, when Pope Pius IX was temporarily exiled from Rome at the very time when much of Europe was convulsed by radical unrest. This was regarded as a fulfilment of prophecy.

It is also important not to regard Catholicism, or more especially Protestantism, as a monolithic block. The assertion of dogmatic Ultramontanism was not achieved without internal tension, which manifested itself above all in those parts of the Catholic world, notably France, which had traditionally maintained a degree of freedom from papal authority (an outlook known as Gallicanism). Moreover the anti-clericalism – hostility to the institutional church and its clergy – which was prominent in many Catholic countries during the period, should not necessarily be seen as anti-religious, but rather as reflecting an aspiration to reconstruct Catholicism itself on a more rational and less hierarchical basis. On the Protestant side of the fence, divisions went back to the Reformation itself and had been reinforced in the intervening centuries. By the nineteenth century the historical divisions of Calvinist and Arminian, Anglican, Lutheran and Anabaptist, had been overlaid by a newer set of tensions flowing from the Evangelical awakening of the mid-eighteenth century which profoundly influenced Protestant communities from the Elbe to the Hebrides. The emphasis of Evangelical leaders such as Nikolaus von Zinzendorf (1700–60) and John Wesley (1703–91) on direct experiential encounter with God was a powerful solvent of more doctrinally rigid and institutionalized versions of Protestantism. The implications extended outside the religious sphere in that the growth of new intense religious movements outside the established structure of state churches changed the nature of civil society and the mechanisms by which political control could be exercised. No longer could governments rely on all or most of their people belonging to a single state church. Given that substantial groups remained very committed to their religious convictions, this growing pluralism gave rise to significant tensions.

A transitional period ensued until (as described in Unit 2) the structures of secular liberal states in which religion was increasingly marginalized became firmly established around the end of the nineteenth century. In the meantime however religious issues could assume considerable political importance: for example in Britain, from early nineteenth-century demands for civil equality from Roman Catholics and Nonconformists to early twentieth-century disputes over the role of the churches in state education. A further stimulus to division and change within Protestantism was the development of liberal and sceptical religious thought. These currents flowed in part from the legacy of the eighteenth-century Enlightenment, but were reinforced by the growing pace of historical and scientific investigation during the nineteenth century. Moreover the impact of such general spiritual, cultural and intellectual trends cut across numerous other factors which heightened the diversity of European religion, in Catholic as in Protestant areas. Differences between the social experience of town and country, between places experiencing rapid change and those which were relatively stable, between clergy and laity, educated and illiterate, rich and poor, all were reflected in religious life.

We shall pursue these points further shortly. First however, it is helpful to pause briefly to try to picture the map of religious affiliation across Europe and to ponder its significance. The heartland of Protestantism was in that region of central Europe east of the Rhine, west of the Vistula and north of the Alps that corresponds to Germany, the Netherlands, and part of Switzerland. Especially towards the south of that area the patchwork of local affiliation becomes bewilderingly complex, with adjoining principalities and cantons holding different confessional allegiances and predominantly Protestant towns surrounded by predominantly Catholic countryside. The nearer to the Baltic and the North Sea one looks the more Protestantism appeared in the ascendant, a pattern continued further north and west in Scandinavia, Great Britain and the north-eastern corner of Ireland. In Poland, to the east, the majority of the population was Catholic – and national identity tended to be defined very much in Catholic terms (cf. Norman Davies on Video 3) – but there were substantial Protestant, Jewish, Orthodox and Uniate minorities. Meanwhile, to the south, and south west, Catholicism predominated, although sometimes with conspicuous Protestant minorities, notably in France, southern Ireland and north-western Italy. The most exclusively Catholic parts of Europe were Spain, Portugal and southern Italy.

Exercise   Now please turn to Offprint 10. As you read the extract answer the following three questions:

1   What were the main consequences and implications of popular Protestant movements?

2   Under what circumstances and for what reasons did opposition to traditional Christianity develop?

3   Why was the Catholic Church generally more successful in combating secularizing trends than were Protestants?

Specimen Answers and   1   The cultural and social impact of such movements could be very sub-
Discussion   stantial, drawing as they did on folk religion and consciousness, as
                            well as on the teachings of orthodox Christianity. Their appeal was
                            primarily but not exclusively to 'the common people' and hence

ensured that Christian conviction was by no means a monopoly of the educated, wealthy and powerful. Indeed, McLeod implies, religious influences played an important part in the development of community and class consciousness at the lower levels of society, albeit not so much among those right at the bottom of the pile. In the long run, however, popular Protestant movements tended to divide communities as well as to unite them: not everyone felt happy with the strict, often teetotal culture and morality of the religiously committed. (You should note, incidentally, how heavily dependent McLeod's account here is on British evidence: he suggests that similar processes were at work in Germany, the Netherlands and Scandinavia, but does not provide detailed examples to support his case.)

2 The key point here is that, at the grass-roots, institutional rivalry and its sociological impact was more significant than abstract ideological confrontation. It was true that anti-clerical groups, whether Freemasons, positivists or socialists, had ideas which were at odds with traditional Christian ones, but their rivalry with the churches was developed in specific conflicts over education and the provision of social and cultural institutions for the working classes. They did not so much, in an intellectual sense, convince men and women that Christianity was no longer credible, as provide them with alternative social structures which meant that for many the churches were no longer at the centre of community life.

3 The ability of Ultramontane Catholicism to combine a 'highly dogmatic and anti-rationalist theology with a warmly emotional piety' made it very effective among relatively poorly educated people. Its power was reinforced by the cultivation of popular devotion to the Blessed Virgin, by a resurgence in the numbers and power of the religious orders, by control over the education of the children of the faithful and by use of the press. You may well feel that McLeod gives you less help in explaining relative Protestant failure, but I hope that you were able to draw out the inference that lack of visible unity, a more dispersed authority structure, and less capacity to appeal to popular supernaturalism (once the enthusiasm of the revivals had subsided) were significant sources of weakness.

One general impression I hope you will have derived from your reading of McLeod is the substantial importance of the relationship between religion and community. Religious revival played a key role in forming new structures of community; a tightly-knit community in which the institutional church provided essential social and cultural services was likely to have high levels of religious involvement. Arguably, the Catholic Church was the most successful of nineteenth-century religious bodies in forming and sustaining such links with the social fabric, but the point can be further illustrated by a glance at the Protestant churches in Britain. On the one hand were the Established state churches, Anglican in England and Wales and Presbyterian in Scotland, which divided the land up into parishes, and were bound up with traditional social and political structures. They could maintain a dominant position in communities where authority and geography were on their side, for example in compact rural villages with a resident squire, in some English cathedral cities; and even in industrial areas if they had the support of the leading employers. An awareness of the importance of community in sustaining religious observance was apparent in the anxiety of church reformers to create and endow new parishes which, it was hoped, would become the bases for stronger communities than were possible in existing large and unwieldy parishes.

On the other hand was Nonconformity which gained dramatically increased support from the 1790s onwards, partly, as McLeod emphasizes, because of the appeal of popular evangelicalism to lower-class communities, but also because of its important role in providing an ideology and a sense of distinctive identity for the urban industrial and commercial middle class (Davidoff and Hall, 1987). Furthermore, Nonconformity had considerable political significance: demands for civil equality were an important contributor to the growth of liberalism, which culminated in the Gladstonian era of the last third of the nineteenth century.

Such Protestant dimensions are vital for an overall understanding of the important formative role of religion in nineteenth-century European society and politics, but in order to give some focus to the remainder of this part of the unit, I have chosen to concentrate on two contrasting case studies relating to primarily Catholic countries. In particular, the examination of France will enable us to explore the implications of revolutionary political change for the situation of religion, while the case of Ireland will illuminate both the implications of vigorous religious competition between Protestants and Catholics, and the relationships between religion and national consciousness.

France: Catholicism and revolution

France was, as I have already noted, in terms of its organized religious observance primarily a Roman Catholic country. However, events shortly before the outset of our period raised in an acute form the question of whether that nominal allegiance corresponded to the underlying convictions and experience of the French nation. During the eighteenth century, the French Enlightenment had assumed a tone notably critical of traditional religion, a standpoint reflected above all in the works of Voltaire. It was though the unfolding of revolution in the years after 1789 that really seemed to weaken the position of the Church. During a short space of time the Church found itself stripped of its extensive wealth – it had owned ten per cent of French land before the Revolution – and its clergy were bitterly divided against each other and against the state by the requirement (in 1790) that they should swear an oath accepting civil authority over them. Many refused. As the Revolution entered its later more radical phases substantial numbers of clergy were executed, massacred and deported. Eventually, in late 1793 and early 1794, there was an outright onslaught against Catholicism which led to the temporary closure of the great majority of churches, while most of the clergy either emigrated or ceased to practise their priestly functions.

The phase of radical 'dechristianization', as it was called did not last long and, in 1801, Napoleon agreed a Concordat with the Pope. This restored a functioning Catholic hierarchy in France, but one much more subordinate to the secular state than the pre-revolutionary Church had been. The clergy were now paid by the state. The restoration of the Bourbons in 1815 brought a political climate still more favourable to the Church: recruitment to the clergy grew and popular religious fervour appears to have increased. After the Revolution of 1830 the pendulum swung back again somewhat: Louis Philippe's government was less favourable to Catholicism than those of Louis XVIII and Charles X had been. However the turmoil of the 1848 Revolution and the short-lived Second Republic heightened the attractions of Catholicism as a source of order and stability in the country, an association exploited by Napoleon III during the Second Empire. The writer and diplomat Gustave de Beaumont bemoaned in 1862 the 'ignorant, unreflecting character of the French peasantry'. 'But', he went on 'if our peasants lose their religion, they will become savages. It is their only restraint, their only intellectual exercise. Their intercourse with the priest alone raises them above barbarism' (Senior, 1880, I, p.196).

After 1870 the Third Republic saw yet another distinct phase in relations between religion and the French state. Initially – as illustrated in the enthusiasm for the Sacré-Coeur project which had the support of the National Assembly – sympathy for Catholicism was strong, but as time went on government policy became increasingly secular and anti-clerical in orientation. The competing endeavours of Church and government to control the education of the young were a particular focus of confrontation. During the 1890s Pope Leo XIII encouraged French Catholics to come to a degree of accommodation with the Republic in the so-called Ralliement. This movement had some limited success but it was essentially swimming against the tide: in 1905 came the Separation of Church and State implying the ending of the century-long endeavour to reconcile Catholicism with the Revolution.

Underlying the bewildering changes and reversals of nineteenth-century French history was then an underlying conflict of two ways of expressing national identity, the one secular, revolutionary, and republican; the other Catholic, conservative, and often royalist. As the contemporary historian Jules Michelet put it, there were 'two principles, two actors and two persons, Christianity and the Revolution' (quoted in Ford, 1993, p.6). The consciousness of confrontation shaped the behaviour of both sides. Even as the trauma of the 1790s passed out of living memory, the church could not forget that the Revolution had once threatened its very existence; republican leaders, for their part, remained profoundly suspicious of the Church's potential to be a focus for counter-revolution. Such fear of counter-revolution was also bound up with a sense that the national integrity of France was threatened, whether from the international influence of the papacy, or from the regionalist inclinations of strongly Catholic areas, notably Brittany.

Exercise   I should now like you to look at two first-hand impressions of Catholicism in nineteenth-century France, one (Document III.6) from the English economist Nassau Senior who attended a service at Notre Dame in Paris in March 1862; the other (Document III.7) from the Irish Bishop of Ossory, William Kinsella, who described his impressions on a visit in 1828 to the French writer Alexis de Torqueville. Note that both these accounts relate to periods when government attitudes to Catholicism were relatively favourable, the Bourbon Restoration and the Second Empire. Bearing this in mind, what do you think we can learn from these extracts about the strengths and weaknesses of the French Church in this period? What were the advantages and disadvantages of connection with the state?

Discussion   The strength indicated by both documents is the continuing extent of popular support for Catholicism. Kinsella observes that 'religion seems to have deep roots in France. It still has a hold on the people'. Senior's account of Notre Dame gives unwitting testimony to the same point, in the allusion to the crowded state of the cathedral, with a congregation which the writer estimates at 'three or four thousand'. (Such indications for mid-nineteenth-century Paris are all the more striking as it was in fact one of the least religiously-fervent parts of the country.)

Senior's account, however, also draws attention to a significant weakness, the sense, as indicated at least in the views of this particular preacher, of being wholly at odds with important intellectual currents of the time. As Senior points out, the juxtaposition of reason and faith made faith appear dangerously isolated and insubstantial, at least to educated people.

As my question implies, I think that the Church–State connection, as discussed by Kinsella, had ambivalent implications. If you thought that Kinsella's views were telling you as much about his native Ireland as about France, you would have picked up an important aspect of this document. We shall return to the Irish case shortly. In the meantime however, you might have reflected on how, despite Kinsella's reservations, public support from the government was obviously important to the Church in re-establishing its influence after the disruption of the Revolution. On the other hand, as Kinsella points out, a state-supported Church might find it very difficult to identify with the aspirations and concerns of the common people. That might have led you on to the speculation that the loosening of this between Church and state in the later nineteenth and early twentieth centuries perhaps brought gains as well as losses for the Church, in terms of its popular appeal. This hypothesis does indeed have some support from hard historical evidence.

In addition to the polarity of Catholicism and Revolution, Church and state, the other key feature of French religion in the nineteenth century that I want you to understand is its sheer diversity. It is very important that you avoid stereotyped images of a 'French Catholic'. One important aspect of this diversity was geographical. Look at the map (Fig. 9) showing the religious vitality of French dioceses in 1877, which indicates that the good areas (from the Catholic Church's point of view) were the east from Lorraine down to the Alps, the southern Massif Central, the Pyrenees, Brittany, and the extreme north. Religious vitality was lowest in the region around Paris, particularly to the south east of the capital. The extremes of religious observance (as measured by those taking Easter Communion) were remarkable: in 1909 the figure was 8.1 per cent for the diocese of Chartres (in the centre of the country to the south-west of Paris); in 1912 it was 95.2 per cent for the diocese of St Brieuc in northern Brittany

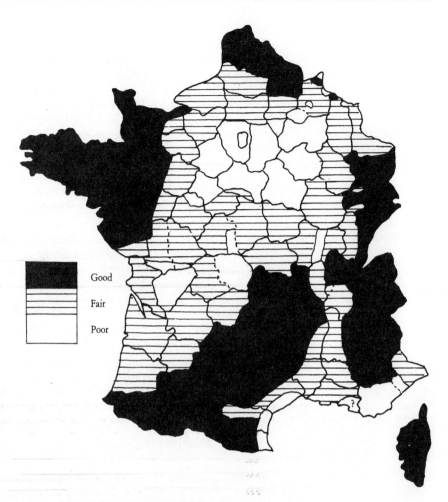

Good

Fair

Poor

Figure 9
Religious vitality of French
dioceses in 1877: estimate
of religious practice by
bishops and prefects. From
Ralph Gibson, A Social
History of French
Catholicism 1789–1914.
(London, Routledge, 1989)

(Gibson, 1989, pp.174–5). While it is true that the more fervent Catholic areas were generally the more remote and rural parts of the country, there was no straightforward correlation between religious practice and socio-economic development. Levels of observance could vary very markedly between districts which were quite close together, notably between southern Brittany and the *départements* to the south of it; and between the Mediterranean coast and its hinterland.

Moreover such regional differences were astonishingly enduring – their origins can be traced to the eighteenth century and before – and they were still very much apparent in the mid-twentieth century. The implication accordingly is that religion was very much a product and reflection of the diversities of regional history and culture. (A similar picture, incidentally, existed elsewhere in Europe, notably in Britain. When levels of church attendance there, measured in 1851, are plotted on a map, the result is a patchwork quilt very reminiscent of the French one you have in front of you.)

A second key factor relating to religious observance in nineteenth-century France was gender. The invariable pattern was for women to be more observant than men: for example in the diocese of Périgeux in the

Dordogne in 1841 71.4 per cent of women but only 25.3 per cent of men took communion at Easter (Gibson, 1989, p.175). This gender difference was also reflected in recruitment to religious orders, which, incidentally, enjoyed increasing numbers from both sexes for much of the nineteenth century. In 1878 there were 30,000 members of male religious orders, but nearly 130,000 female 'religeuses' (not necessarily 'nuns' in the traditional sense – many of them had much less strictly regulated lives) (Gibson, 1989, p.108).

Exercise   Can you think of reasons for these gender contrasts?

Discussion   Three points occur to me, the first two of which I hope you might have thought of, but the third of which does require some further background knowledge of French Catholicism.

1   I am very suspicious of assertions that women are 'naturally' more religious than men. Nevertheless, in a society where medical knowledge was still very limited, key features of women's biological experience still seemed deeply mysterious. Above all childbirth remained an unpredictable and potentially very dangerous undertaking, which meant that even young healthy women had good cause to reflect on the possible imminence of death. Such factors very probably predisposed women to a religious outlook.

2   The church offered women opportunities for social contact and (in the case of the religious orders) something approaching a 'career', which were otherwise not available to them. Men on the other hand had numerous other avenues for employment and sociability.

3   The nineteenth-century French Catholic clergy appears to have been obsessed with the regulation of sexuality and, in particular, with discouraging contraception. *Coitus interruptus* was widely used, and the priests held the man rather than the woman responsible. Thus while women were absolved in the confessional and hence admitted to communion, men tended to give up confession, knowing that they would be likely to be subjected to embarrassingly intimate enquiries (Stengers, 1971). (Do not worry if you did not think of that one!, but if you suspected that differing attitudes to male and female sexuality were somehow significant you were very much on the right lines.)

A third aspect of religious variation was the very different concepts of what it meant to be a Catholic current among Frenchmen and Frenchwomen. At a minimal level it meant that one had been baptized and married in church and expected in due course to have a Christian burial. At its fullest extent Catholic commitment meant participation in a rich range of devotion that could easily become the dominant purpose of an individual's life. Cutting across such degrees of fervour was the distinction between the official Catholicism taught by the clergy and the often very different belief held by the people. The French countryside was still believed to be peopled with a strange assortment of sometimes cantankerous local saints, seen as a source of aid in the various trials and misfortunes of life. Belief in witchcraft and demons was common. To some extent the Church successfully adapted to appeal to those who held such alternative beliefs: for example the tremendous success of the Pyrenean town of Lourdes as a pilgrimage centre in the late nineteenth century derived in part at least from its appeal to those who had traditionally sought cures of illness and spiritual comfort from more local and less orthodox centres of pilgrimage.

So the more closely one looks at French Catholicism, as at any nineteenth-century religious group, the more problematic generalizations become. I hope however that on gaining a brief insight into its sheer diversity and complexity you will be encouraged to think about how religion relates to other aspects of social and cultural history.

Ireland: Religion and national mobilization

Nineteenth-century Ireland was like France, a predominantly Roman Catholic country, but in most other respects its religious history differed markedly. For one thing, levels of participation were much higher than in all but the most devout parts of France: among the Catholic population at least church attendance appears to have been quite close to universal in the late nineteenth century. Also very significant was the political context in which organized religion operated: whereas France was one of the major European powers, Ireland in this period was a nation without statehood. Between 1800 and 1921 Ireland lacked any parliamentary institutions of its own and was administered essentially as a British government department. In this respect Ireland serves as a relatively unusual western European example of processes more widespread in central and eastern Europe as religious distinctiveness proved to be a major spur to nationalism in countries historically dominated by imperial powers. Catholic Poland's growing defiance of Orthodox Russia and Protestant Prussia, and Orthodox Serbia's resurgence against Catholic Austria and Muslim Turkey are in this respect notable parallels to the case of Ireland.

Ireland, moreover, differed from France in respect of the size and importance of its Protestant minority. Although individual Protestants could achieve considerable prominence, it was irreligion rather than Protestantism which was much the more obvious alternative to Catholicism in nineteenth-century France. In Ireland on the other hand, where in 1861 Catholics made up 77.7 per cent of the population, of the remaining 22.3 per cent, only 146 individuals identified themselves as having no religion, and only a few hundred were Jews. All of the remainder identified with a Protestant denomination (Connolly, 1985, pp.3–6). There was also pronounced regional variation in the distribution of Protestants and Catholics: although in the nineteenth century the concentration of Protestants in the north-eastern part of Ireland was not quite as great as it was to become in the twentieth century, it was still very much apparent. In France, by contrast, there was no part of the country where Protestants were in a majority, as they were in Ireland in the town of Belfast and the four counties of Antrim, Armagh, Down and Londonderry.

Despite their relatively small numbers, Irish Protestants well reflected the diversity and fluidity of the non-Catholic religious world. About half of them identified with the Church of Ireland which, like the Church of England, represented an Anglican Church order and theology. Until 1870 the Church of Ireland was an established church, meaning that it had formal links with the British state, notably in the possession of historic endowments and in the fact that some of its bishops sat in the House of Lords in London. In 1870, the Church of Ireland was disestablished as a gesture towards the Roman Catholic majority. It continued, however, to be associated with the privileged land-owning, socially dominant classes and in that respect was similar to other Protestant state churches, whether Lutheran, Anglican or Calvinist in theology, across northern and central Europe. The next largest Protestant group were the Presbyterians, 9 per cent of the total population of Ireland in 1861 (as compared with the Anglican 12%), and there were small but still noticeable numbers of Methodists, Congregationalists, Baptists and Unitarians. You need not worry about the distinctive characteristics of all these groups: the essential point I want you to note is the importance of avoiding a stereotyped image of an Irish (or any) Protestant: there were numerous different varieties of Protestantism. That diversity was increased by the impact of popular evangelical movements of the kind described by Hugh McLeod in Offprint 10. A notable resurgence of conversionist religious excitement occurred in the Ulster revival of 1859, which heightened the intensity of Protestantism in the province for the remainder of the century.

Protestantism was also important in Ireland out of proportion to its numbers because of its social and political ascendancy, which was very considerable in the early nineteenth century, although it weakened as the period went on. For a Protestant perspective on the Irish religious situation in the 1820s please read the following extract from a personal letter, dated 22 December 1824, from Charles Forster, an Anglican writing from Limerick, to his friend Sir Robert Inglis, in London.

> At present the R.C. population in Ireland, while formidable as compared with the number of souls in the Island, is insignificant when contrasted with the population of the Empire [i.e. the United Kingdom as a whole]. It is strong enough to act as a drag-chain, and no more. Let it be held, politically, within due bounds, and all will be well and as it should be.
>
> But what are these bounds? I would say such as may secure to the Protestants of Ireland a counterpoise to the numerical superiority of their R.C. fellow-subjects. Anything short of this is to abandon the helm to Popery altogether.
>
> *To balance the opposite communions* is the true policy for England: and this balance can be preserved only by continuing to the Protestant community in Ireland such a political preponderance, as will compensate their deficiency in numbers. In a word you must secure to them a Protestant Church Establishment, Protestant representatives, a Protestant judicature, – advantages which will amply compensate any disparity of numbers. When taken in connexion with their possessions of $^{19}/_{20}$ths of the landed property of the Island ... But to charge us with looking for ascendancy is unjust: we claim only *that* weight for property, for intelligence for moral and intellectual cultivation, to which they are entitled in every well-regulated state ...
>
> The plain truth is, the struggle in Ireland is not one of party against party, or creed against creed. It is a struggle of the lower against the upper order of society, of the many against the few.... In Ireland it *happens* that the upper ranks are Protestant, and the lower ranks Roman Catholic. Of this accidental fact, much advantage

has been made by those whose trade it is to trouble mankind ... And this much will I say, that resistance to the claims of the Roman Catholics generally, is the only means left to keep the lower orders in Ireland in their proper place, – in other words to prevent revolution in its worst and most appalling form. (MS letter in Inglis Papers, Canterbury Cathedral Library)

This extract is a striking illustration of the unselfconscious ease with which conservative thinkers in the nineteenth century could defend social inequality as the natural order of things. For our present purposes it also demonstrates well how religion could become implicated in such social and political conflicts. It may well strike you as ironic that Catholicism was feared as revolutionary in Ireland at exactly the same period as it was operating as a key support of counter-revolution in France, but as Forster points out, such alignments were essentially an accidental result of the wider historical circumstances.

Irish Roman Catholicism, too, changed much during the course of the nineteenth century. As in France, Ultramontanism became increasingly influential, but in Ireland the transition was so marked that it has been labelled a 'devotional revolution' (Larkin, 1972). The pivotal event was the Great Famine of 1845–7, the disaster that left hundreds of thousands of people dead and caused millions to emigrate. The population dropped from 8.2 million in 1841 to 4.4 million in 1911. Before the famine the Irish countryside had been crowded with people, often desperately poor, but possessing a vibrant popular culture which was frequently in tension with the teaching of official Catholicism. Meanwhile the Church itself, although increasingly energetic and well organized, simply lacked sufficient clergy to sustain an effective ministry throughout the population. After the famine, however, the Church's resources were more compatible with the demands placed upon them, and popular traditional beliefs were weakened by the massive psychological and social shock of such extensive mortality and migration. Accordingly it became easier for priests to discipline their parishioners into official forms of Catholic belief and practice.

In order to gain a more specific impression of the role of the churches in pre-Famine Irish society, now please read Document III.7, Alexis de Torqueville's account of his visit to the Roman Catholic priest and the Church of Ireland clergyman in a village in the west of Ireland in 1835.

Exercise 1 How would you characterize the differences in the situation of the priest and the clergyman?

2 What are the implications for the development of Irish politics and national consciousness?

Specimen Answers and Discussion 1 Both men have considerable status, but the nature of that status differs substantially. The Catholic priest appears to be known to everyone and to be treated with great respect by them. His living conditions are superior to those of his parishioners – a 'large piece of salmon' is, after all, not *so* modest a meal! Nevertheless, his material circumstances are obviously inferior to those of his Church of Ireland counterpart, with his piano-playing daughter, officer son and social ties with the aristocracy. You might also have reflected in this connection on the implications of the Catholic priest being unmarried and so being single-mindedly committed to his pastoral work. Clearly in this particular village, even before the Famine, the Roman Catholic Church was exercising a very effective ministry. On the other hand the Church of Ireland clergyman was ministering to a small clique of landlords and their servants, sustaining a minority community isolated from the majority of people in the district. I must remind you, however, that the picture would have been different in other parts of Ireland. Connaught, to which this document relates, was one of the most predominantly Catholic parts of the country: in Ulster and along the east coast a Protestant clergyman would have been ministering to a wider cross-section of the population.

2   Pastoral concern for the wretched conditions of his parishioners draws the Roman Catholic priest into political engagement, notably here in relation to the problem of unemployment and in relation to education. This priest, at least, could eventually become an important leader of his community. On the other hand, the Church of Ireland clergyman, despite the short-term resources of wealth and prestige available to him, appears in the long term to be in a dangerously isolated position depending on the support of a landowning class which itself is seen as alien and oppressive. Accordingly hostility to British rule could very readily become bound up with religious antagonism to Protestantism.

Certainly, there is much in the history of nineteenth-century Ireland to illustrate the importance of the link between Roman Catholicism and nationalism. On several occasions, issues centrally concerned with religion became a focus for much more broadly based national self-assertion. An important example of this process was the campaign for Catholic Emancipation led by Daniel O'Connell which culminated in 1829 with the concession to otherwise qualified Roman Catholics of the right to vote in parliamentary elections. The pattern was continued, as I have noted, from the 1830s to the 1860s by the campaign against the privileged status of the Church of Ireland. During the 1830s a particular focus of popular unrest was the tithes traditionally levied on the produce of agriculture to support the Church and bitterly resented by Roman Catholic farmers. A reform in 1838 took much of the sting out of this issue. Meanwhile, the Roman Catholic Church was an important agent of political mobilization even in relation to issues which did not have an obviously religious dimension. Its role was particularly notable in the early 1840s when O'Connell pursued a large-scale campaign for the repeal of the legislative union with Britain. Priests played an important role in generating support in the localities, while the large-scale meetings which were a prominent feature of the movement were evidently designed to appeal to Catholic religious sensibilities. Much later, in the final years of British rule in southern Ireland, the leaders of the Easter Rising of 1916 were stirred by fervent Catholicism, and the Church returned the compliment by becoming even more strongly committed to the cause of independence.

Nevertheless, it is important not to over-simplify the picture. Irish nationalism had a secular dimension too, and while Daniel O'Connell might identify with the Catholic Church he ultimately sought to transcend it in building an Ireland which could incorporate Protestants as well. When he died in 1847, some mourning verses well captured the mixture of ideals and aspirations that lay behind support for him. The first verse evokes Ireland in religiously neutral terms, which could in theory at least incorporate all creeds; the second, however, conveys a more specifically Catholic emphasis.

> Oh Erin, darling, both night and morning
> Your grief's alarming as may be seen;
> Your hills and mountains your silver fountains
> From sweet Killarney to College Green
> Thro' Groves and vallies – thro' lanes and alleys
> Oh bid your children to deplore
> In lamentation; throughout the nation
> Brave O'Connell he is no more ...

> With Christian beauty he did his duty
> for forty years if I say more
> His precious heart he has bequeathed
> In his dying moments to the Church of Rome
> He lived a Christian and died a Martyr
> I well may say for sweet Erin's shore
> Through meditation and contemplation
> His days were ended – he is no more.'

(Trinity College Library, Dublin, Irish Ballads Collection, No. 142, with spelling modernized)

O'Connell's directions on his death bed at Genoa that his heart should be taken on to Rome and his body taken back to Dublin well symbolized the ambivalences in the relationship between Catholicism and Irish nationalism. A similar point is illustrated in a different way by the career of the most prominent nationalist leader of the later nineteenth century, Charles Stewart Parnell. Parnell, it is worth emphasizing, was a nominal member of the Church of Ireland, although the majority of his fellow Protestants especially in Ulster, opposed his campaign for Home Rule. The Roman Catholic Church, for its part, was generally ready to support Parnell until in 1890 he was cited as co-respondent in a divorce suit. The nationalist movement was badly split by this development, with the Catholic hierarchy refusing to continue support for a man found wanting in the moral sphere, while many ordinary Catholics continued loyal to Parnell until he died in late 1891.

It would therefore be a mistake to see the divided political map of twentieth-century Ireland as an inevitable consequence of the divided religious map of the nineteenth century. For one thing Roman Catholic support for nationalism was by no means unconditional, for another by no means all Protestants were uncompromising advocates of the Union with Britain. That acknowledged, however, the Irish experience in the nineteenth century still serves as a telling illustration of the social importance of religion and its power as a channel of political and national mobilization.

Conclusion

It will be helpful quickly to summarise the main insights I hope that you will have got out of the brief examination of religion in nineteenth-century Europe.

1   Religion was an important and influential force. This does not mean that everyone was a committed believer, although in some parts of Europe at certain times outward observance at least was quite close to universal. What it does mean was that religious (and explicitly anti-religious) forces often weighed heavily in political calculations and social organization.

2   Religious life in nineteenth-century Europe was very diverse. Not only did countries differ from each other, but so did regions within the same country; towns contrasted with country; men with women. Expressions of both Catholicism and Protestantism could vary widely. In the context of this course you do not need to worry about the details of such diversity, but you do need to appreciate that it existed and resist the temptation to engage in crude generalizations about religion.

3   Religion was an integral part of the other processes of historical change, and is very relevant to the concerns of the historian concerned primarily with secular factors. In particular, I have highlighted the role of religion in relation to national identity, in France in providing an alternative to a republican secular concept of the nation; in Ireland in providing a pivot of resistance to British rule.

References

Anderson, P. (1994), *The Printed Image and the Transformation of Popular Culture, 1790–1860*, Clarendon Press, Oxford.

Benoist, J. (1992), *Le Sacré-Coeur de Montmartre de 1870 à nos jours*, Editions Ouvrières, Paris.

Blanning, T.C.W. (1985), 'The role of religion in European counter-revolution, 1789–1815', in D. Beales and G. Best (eds), *History, Society and the Churches*, Cambridge University Press, Cambridge, pp. 195–214.

Connolly, S.J. (1985), *Religion and Society in Nineteenth–Century Ireland*, Dundalgon Press, Dundalk.

Curran, J. (1977), 'Capitalism and control of the press, 1800–1975', in Curran, James, Gurevitch, Michael, and Woollacott (eds), *Mass Communication and Society*, Edward Arnold, London, pp.195–230.

Davidoff, L. and Hall, C. (1987), *Family Fortunes: Men and Women of the English Middle Class 1780–1850*, Hutchinson, London.

Ford, C. (1993), *Creating the Nation in Provincial France: Religion and Political Identity in Brittany*, Princeton University Press, Princeton.

Gibson, R. (1989), *A Social History of French Catholicism 1789–1914*, Routledge, London.

Gildea, R. (1991), *Barricades and Borders, Europe 1800-1914*, Oxford University Press, Oxford.

Harris, J. (1993), *Private Lives, Public Spirit. A Social History of Britain, 1870–1914*, Oxford University Press, Oxford.

Larkin, E. (1972), 'The Devotional Revolution in Ireland, 1850–75', *American Historical Review*, 77, pp. 625–52.

Senior, N.W. (1880), *Conversations with Distinguished Persons during the Second Empire*, edited by M.C.M. Simpson 2 vols, London.

Stengers, J. (1971), 'Les Pratiques anti-conceptionelles dans le mariage au XIXeme et au XXeme siècles: Problemes humains et attitudes religeuses', *Revue belge de philologie et d'histoire*, no. 49, pp.403–81.

Texier, E. (1852) *Tableau de Paris*, 2 vols, Paris.

Unit 15
State and economy in the creation of nation

Prepared for the course team by Richard Bessel

Contents

Study timetable

Weeks of Study	Texts	Video	AC
2	Unit 15; Anderson, Chapter 4; Offprints 11, 12	Video 3	

You should also view again TV3 as you work through this unit.

Aim

The aim of this unit is to help you understand how 'nations' and nation-states were created in nineteenth-century Europe.

Objectives

By the end of this unit you should be able to discuss:

1   the contribution of state structures and economic development to the formation of national consciousness in nineteenth-century Europe;

2   the role of state structures and economic development in the unification of Germany and Italy;

3   how and why national consciousness developed among 'nations' without states.

Introduction

> I am not worried that Germany does not become one; our good high-ways and future railways will surely do their work. (Johann Wolfgang Goethe, 1828, to Johann Peter Eckermann; quoted in Treue, 1979, p.217)
> A state can sometimes create a nation, but for a nation to create a state is going against nature. (Lord Acton (from his 1862 essay on 'Nationality', in *History of Freedom and other Essays*, London, 1907; quoted in Davies, 1982, p.3)

The growth of national consciousness and the creation of European nation-states were among the most important developments in the nineteenth century, and developments which we tend to take for granted today. The same may be said for complex and interventionist bureaucratic state structures and for dynamic industrial economies, as you have seen from the previous two blocks of this course. The purpose of this unit is to examine how these themes may be linked, and thus to attempt to explain the development of 'nation' and 'nationalism' in nineteenth-century Europe. But in doing so we should not assume conclusions before we reach them: we cannot simply assume that state organization and economic structures necessarily were what created European 'nations' and bound them together in the nine-teenth century. The links need to be questioned and demonstrated, not merely assumed; our questions need to be open, not set up to lead us towards pre-determined conclusions.

Like most of the themes in this course, the theme of this unit is not one which has faded away since the end of the nineteenth century. In a European Union, in which nationalism promises to redraw political maps and threatens the political integrity of a number of member countries, and in a post-cold-war Europe, in which nationalism has reared its head in often virulent and dangerous forms, the questions posed here are of obvi-ous contemporary importance. We are still, perhaps more than ever, hav-ing to grapple with the legacies of the nineteenth century.

The creation of nations in nineteenth-century Europe: some examples

Germany and Poland

In 1831, four years before the first German railway was opened (between Nuremberg and Fürth, in Franconia in the kingdom of Bavaria), the national economist Friedrich List published a plan for a national railway network . List was both a great publicist for a German customs union and a great enthusiast for the railway. (Friedrich List is discussed in Anderson, pp.230–1.) As List envisaged the future, Berlin would become the focus of a vast national railway network, linking the Prussian (and future German) capital with Hamburg, Hannover, Cologne, Frankfurt/Main, Leipzig, Dresden, Munich, Stettin, Prague, Danzig and Breslau. (See map in Pounds, 1985, p.455.) At the time when List was writing, it should be remembered, Berlin was the capital of Prussia, Hamburg a city-state, Hannover the capital of the Kingdom of Hannover, Dresden the capital of the Kingdom of Saxony and Leipzig the major Saxon commercial centre, Munich the capital of the Kingdom of Bavaria, Cologne in the Rhineland (recently annexed by Prussia) and Prague under Habsburg rule in the Austrian Empire. 'Germany' may have been a 'nation' in the eyes of Fichte and List, but as a political unit – as a 'nation-state' – it did not yet exist.

As things turned out, the German Customs Union of 1834 and the railway network, the construction of which began with the Nuremberg–Fürth line in 1835, predated the unified German Empire proclaimed in the Hall of Mirrors at Versailles on 18 January 1871. At the beginning of the nineteenth century, it was uncertain just what 'Germany' was (and most German speakers probably did not care), and the differences in dialect, customs and consciousness between, for example, Catholics in Baden or Upper Bavaria and Protestants in Pomerania or Hamburg were enormous. On the eve of the First World War, however, while the differences remained substantial, 'Germany' effectively had been defined (as the 'little Germany' – excluding Austria – of Bismarck's Reich) and 'German' consciousness sufficiently developed for millions of men from Munich to Memel to march off to war for Kaiser and Fatherland.

Germany thus appears to offer the classic example for a discussion of the importance of state and economy in the creation of 'nation' in nineteenth-century Europe. Germany, as schoolchildren have been informed for over a century, was created by 'blood and iron'; the unified German state of 1871 both became Europe's premier economic power by 1914 and effectively defined what was the German 'nation'. (Remember what Wolfgang Mommsen has to say about this on Video 3.) If any nation may be said to have been a product of economic development and the binding power of a strong state, then that nation most probably was Germany. (We will return to the subject of German national identity below in the section entitled 'Economy and nation', p.120.)

The classic example which turns almost all such generalizations about 'state, economy and nation' generated by German unification on their head is that of Poland. During the long nineteenth century, a Polish state did not exist, the Poles, as Norman Davies has noted, 'belong to a community which has acquired its modern sense of nationality in active opposition to the policies of the states in which they lived' (Davies, 1982, p.11). Between the last partition of Poland in 1795 and the resurrection of an independent Polish state in 1918, Poles lived under Russian, Prussian and Austrian rule – even if they refused to consider themselves 'Russians', 'Prussians' or 'Austrians'. During the nineteenth century they were subjects of the Romanovs, Hohenzollerns and Habsburgs. Their lives were organized by different states in different economic regions.

Even the development of the railways, which served a nation-building function in the German case, tended to divide Poles rather than unite them: Poznan's principal connections were to Berlin, Warsaw's to Moscow and Cracow's to Vienna; and the railway gauge in Russian ('Congress')

'Poland' was different from that in the Prussian and Austrian dominions. However, these obstacles to national unity notwithstanding, it was during the nineteenth century that modern Polish nationalism took shape. There is no question here of 'state and economy' creating a 'nation', but rather of a 'nation' taking shape despite economic divides and state frontiers.

This last caveat is underlined by the example of nineteenth-century Poland. As Anderson notes (p.209), at the outset of the nineteenth century Polish national feeling was 'limited', but by the end of the century it was powerful enough to fuel a successful movement for the reconstitution of a Polish state. Until the partitions, Poland had been a multi-lingual, multi-religious state; the Polish 'nation', such as it was, was limited essentially to a particular social class, the *Szlachta* nobility. This changed fundamentally in the course of the nineteenth century, as the Germans, Belorussians, Lithuanians and Ukrainians in formerly Polish lands came to identify themselves more with others who spoke the same language as they, than with other fellow inhabitants of notionally Polish lands whose language was different. This development left a core of Polish-speaking Catholics, and with the spread of democratic ideas Polish national identity no longer remained limited to a particular economic class; Polish-speaking peasants and workers came increasingly to think of themselves as 'Poles'.

The rise of Polish national consciousness took place against the background of, and in reaction to, restrictions and discrimination aimed against Polish speakers. This has been particularly well-documented in the case of the new German Empire, where following the unification, waves of discrimination and concerted attempts to suppress expressions of Polish national identity were aimed against Polish speakers, as the language of German politics took on an increasingly strident and paranoid anti-Slavic tone. In a cabinet meeting in October 1871 Bismarck asserted:

> From the Russian border to the Adriatic Sea, we are confronted with a Slavic agitation working hand in hand with the Ultramontanes and reactionaries; we must openly defend our national interests and our language against such hostile activities. (Hagen, 1980, p.29)

And, speaking in the Prussian *Landtag* during the following February, the Iron Chancellor claimed that:

> ... the Polish agitation thrives perhaps only because of the benevolence of the government but, I can assure you, there will be no more of it. (Hagen, 1980, p.129)

Words were followed by deeds: Bismarck's anti-Catholic *Kulturkampf* during the 1870s (see Unit 2); the substituting in 1873 of German for Polish as the language of instruction in the schools of the overwhelmingly Polish-speaking Province of Poznan (Posen); the enactment of the Prussian Language Law of 1876, which made German the sole language permitted to be used in the courts and in public administration; the expulsion in 1885 of tens of thousands of Poles who were not Prussian citizens to 'Congress Poland' (in the Russian Empire) and Galicia (in the Habsburg Empire); attempts to promote German settlement in the eastern Prussian provinces at the expense of the Poles; and in 1908 legal restrictions on the use of the Polish language in public assemblies.

These developments signalled a fundamental shift in the nature of politics and the place of national identity within them. In 1896, the Prussian

Culture Minister Robert Bosse informed the Prussian *Landtag* in 1896 that Prussia was:

> ... a German state – not a federal state, which is put together out of individual German, Polish, Danish elements or nationalities; rather we are a German national state. (quoted in Eley, 1986, p.214)

This amounted to an explicit repudiation of the pledge made to Polish speakers by Prussian King Friedrich Wilhelm III in his Poznan Declaration of May 1815:

> You are being incorporated into My Monarchy without having to deny your nationality... Your language is to be used along with German in all public transactions. (quoted in Eley, 1986, p.205)

A new language of politics had taken shape in the course of the nineteenth century: Citizenship was not to be defined just by one's relationship to the state (e.g. as a Prussian subject), but also by one's cultural identity, one's 'nationality' (e.g. as a 'German' or a 'Pole').

The developments outlined above made it increasingly clear to Polish speakers that they were not going to find much favour among Germans. Consequently, and quite contrary to German intentions, Polish speakers responded by identifying themselves increasingly as Poles: by the growth of Polish nationalist cultural and political associations; with the crumbling, during the last two decades before the First World War, of electoral support among Poles in Upper Silesia for the (German) Catholic Centre Party and the corresponding growth of electoral support for Polish nationalists (see Table in Ritter, 1980, p.74); with school strikes over restrictive linguistic policies; and, later, with the outbreak of successful revolutionary Polish nationalism in the eastern Prussian provinces in 1918 and 1919. In the case of the German Empire, the development of a German nation state and economic integration within it obviously did not undermine Poles' sense of their own nationhood vis-à-vis the Germans. However, this is not to say that the development of the state and the economy failed to lead to nation-creation. Indeed, it suggests the opposite: that is, that state interventions and economic developments in the nineteenth century may have lead to nation-creation whatever the political structures involved or the intentions of political élites. That is to say, it may have been the state intervention – trying to force Polish speakers to use German – which provoked national consciousness.

Exercise   Note how Poland is mentioned in Anderson. How would you characterize the way in which Anderson treats Poland, and how would you explain this treatment?

Discussion   The answer to the first part of this question is obvious: Anderson mentions Poland very little, and where he does mention the Poles he tends merely to note Polish nationalism and the unsuccessful revolts against Russian and Tsarist rule (in 1830–1 and 1863). With regard to the second part of the question, it may be that the paucity of Anderson's discussion about Poles and Poland reflects an approach which tends to focus on the nation-state: the discussion is organized largely around nations which were, or became, politically organized in states. 'The Triumph of Nationalism', which provides the first sub-heading for Chapter 4 ('States and Nations'), is viewed not simply as a matter of Europeans coming to identify themselves with national groups in the course of the nineteenth century, but of the development of *nation-states*: here 'nation' becomes the organizing concept for 'state'.

Italy

We began this section by noting that the building of the German railway network predated the unified German Empire (see above, p.107). In the case of the other great national unification of nineteenth-century Europe, that of Italy, it was the other way round. A much more dynamic economic development in some parts of Germany from the late 1850s was reflected in an earlier growth of the railway network there than in the Italian states.

Anderson notes (p.153) that at the time of the 1859 war with Austria (which was the opening round in a series of conflicts which led to a united Italy), there were fewer than 1500 kilometres of track in what became 'Italy'. He then goes on to write that 'by 1864 this had grown sharply, to over 4000 kilometres. The rapid growth was meant, not altogether without success, to stitch together more effectively what was still a deeply divided country.' Here the contribution of the railway network was not one of pre-figuring rather than subsequently consolidating national unification.

Anderson also asserts, on that same page, that 'it is not an accident that so many statesmen who stood for significant political change, normally in a nationalist direction, were strong advocates of railways', pointing to Kossuth in Hungary, Witte in Russia and Cavour in Italy. Count Camillo Benso di Cavour, who from his base in Piedmont did more than perhaps anyone else to make Italian unification a reality, in fact had begun his political career with an article on the significance of railways, expressing the hope that a new communications system would destroy the divisions, 'the petty municipal passions', which divided Italy (Lyttelton, 1993, p.88). (Cavour also was very successful in business, and by 1850 had become the director of a bank and a railway company!) Of course, such a vision did not quite constitute an accurate prediction of how things turned out, and, as Paul Ginsborg observed in the video interview we conducted with him for this course (Video 3), 'some Italian historians would still deny that Italy as a nation exists'. However, for the moment it is of less interest for us here that Italian unification often has been regarded as a botched job than that the belief in the unifying power of railways was so widely accepted in the mid-nineteenth century.

Exercise Unfortunately, Anderson has rather little to say about the tangled processes of Italian unification, but what he does include helps to put our theme here into context. Please now read over Anderson's short outline of the major steps towards Italian unification taken in 1859 and 1860 (pp.20–1). On p.21 Anderson writes of the annexations to Piedmont which created an 'Italy' in 1860: 'This whole process was in an important sense artificial.' Why and how was it 'artificial'?

Discussion Anderson makes this quite clear: the movement for Italian national unity 'was not one of the mass of the population' but 'rather one of the educated, of the urban middle classes and in some areas of the nobility'; the plebiscites which confirmed Italian unity under the Piedmontese king Victor Emmanuel II 'were largely formalities', since only a tiny minority of the population participated in them.

This suggests that for a process of national unification not to be 'artificial' it ought to involve the majority of the population, and not just be an expression of the romantic ideals of an educated élite. It ought perhaps to have deeper social, economic and political roots. In Italy, however, the process was to be the other way round. First 'Italy' was established, and then the state and economic structures which cemented (and were an expression of) national unity would be created. Once that had occurred, then national unification no longer would be 'artificial'.

It is worth considering too the implications of this use of the word 'artificial'. It implies that there is such a thing as a 'natural' process of nation-state formation, one which somehow involves the majority of the population. Does this not silently buy into the nationalist perspective, by assuming that the normal, natural thing is for a nation-state to rest upon broad popular national consciousness (and that the normal, natural thing is for people to consider themselves members of a 'nation')?

From this account at least, it would seem that the Italian unification was done back to front: that – due to the foreign-policy machinations of France's Napoleon III, the sober and calculating diplomacy of the Piedmontese Prime Minister Count Cavour, the military and political weakness of the reactionary Austrian Empire, and the idealism of educated middle-class enthusiasts for Italian unity – first Italy had to be unified and then the preconditions for Italian unification had to be created. That is to say, it was the task of the new Italian nation-state to create the preconditions for its existence. It then was for a new Italian state to weld together Sicilians, Neapolitans, Piedmontese, Tuscans, Calabrians, Venetians and Sardinians into an Italian nation.

Much of the impetus for unification which came among Italian liberal educated and commercial élites stemmed from their sense that this was the way of the future, and that if Italy did not travel down this path then the country would be left behind. In a fine recent survey of 'the national question in Italy', Adrian Lyttelton observes:

> In the new climate of European economic expansion, with railway-building and the extension of free trade, the achievement of these aims took on added urgency. Only the creation of an economic and political federation could prevent Italy from being left at the starting-gate in the race for commercial and industrial progress. It was this perception of the European 'peaceful revolution' and Italy's possible place in it, rather than the pressure of already formed economic interests, which accounts for the popularity of the national economic programme of liberalism. (Lyttelton, 1993, pp.88–9)

Lyttelton goes on to observe that 'it is difficult to disentangle economic and political motives in the "programme for a national opinion" ', and notes that liberals such as Cavour regarded economic unification as a way of achieving their political objectives and of advancing the national cause without having to engage in conspiratorial politics (of the sort pursued by Giuseppe Mazzini). Economic unification would provide the basis for political unification.

Nevertheless, we should not assume that things worked out as hoped or that Italian unification actually did bring about its preconditions. In fact, the historical record is contradictory. (It always is!) For one thing, not all economic interests necessarily were in favour of national unification and free trade; for example, commercial interests in Piedmont feared that their traditional ties with France would be endangered by unification. For another, the north–south divide remained and, perhaps, even intensified. The extension of Piedmontese law, education and centralized bureaucratic structures may have helped tie Italians together in one nation-state, but they also provoked fierce resistance, particularly in the South, where a virtual civil war raged between 1861 and 1865. In December 1860 Cavour's provincial governor of Naples reported on 'the impossibility of founding a government on anything other than force'; the imposition of Piedmontese law and bureaucracy, and the concomitant dismissal of thousands of old-regime officials and tens of thousands of soldiers provided recruits for a guerrilla war against the new state in the South, which in August 1863 was declared to be 'in a state of brigandage' and which was subjected to military law for two years. In Sicily opposition to outside authority, taxation and military conscription by an alien state, which was unable to provide effective administration, gave rise during the 1860s to the network which we know as the Mafia; and in 1866 opposition to Piedmontese policies provoked a major insurrection at Palermo. Far from paving the way for the creation of a national community living in a unified nation-state, as Robert Gildea has observed, Italian 'unification served only to exacerbate regional separatism and to sew the problem into the fabric of the young state' (Gildea, 1987, pp.196–7). Rather than eradicate the tensions and rivalries which formed the background to the dramatic events of 1859–60, unification served to intensify them – with consequences which remain with us today.

The Habsburg Empire

The great loser in the processes of national unification and growing nationalist feeling described above was the Habsburg Empire. German unification under Prussian hegemony was the flip side of the exclusion of Austria from a German confederation in 1866. Slav nationalisms played a major role in undermining the dynastic Habsburg state; and the processes of Italian unification began with the French and the Piedmontese driving the Austrians out of Milan in 1859 and continued with the Austrians (facing the forces of both the Prussians and the Italians) being forced to leave Venetia in 1866. However, it was not only abroad that the Habsburg state found itself on the defensive: soon after their decisive defeat at the hands of the Prussians at Sadowa in 1866, the Austrians were compelled to compromise at home as well, with the 1867 'Ausgleich' (compromise) with the Hungarians, creating the structure of the Austro-Hungarian 'dual monarchy' which collapsed at the end of the First World War.

The 'Ausgleich' which became law in December 1867 was one of the great turning points of nineteenth-century European history. It marked a decisive shift in the basis of the Habsburg monarchy, by destroying the old dynastic principle which hitherto had held it together: 'that all the subject nationalities of the Emperor were equal and that their loyalty to him was its cement' (Gildea, 1987, p.211). Before 1867, one's position in the Habsburg state was determined by one's relationship to the Emperor; afterwards, nationality played an increasingly important role – with ultimately fatal consequences for this vast multi-national empire. After 1867, the monarchy was divided into two: in the eastern Hungarian half, a state nominally headed by the Emperor as 'King of Hungary' but in fact dominated by the Hungarian nobility; in the western Austrian half a federation largely dominated by German speakers. (The Ministers of Foreign Affairs and War, and the budgets of these two ministries, were common to both parts of the monarchy.) Each half of the Dual Monarchy, however, contained large Slav populations: in the Austrian half, Czechs in Bohemia and Moravia, Poles in Galicia, and Slovenes in today's Slovenia; in the Hungarian half, Slovaks and Croats. (See Map 4 in the Maps Booklet which shows the ethnic diversity of the Austro-Hungarian Empire.)

During the last third of the nineteenth century, this configuration proved a recipe for considerable tension. On the one side, there was a growing sense of national identity among Slavs – a sense of being Czech rather than being a subject of the Emperor; on the other side, there was concern by the dominant national and linguistic groups – the Hungarians and the German-speaking Austrians – to contain Slav nationalism. Perhaps the clearest examples of this are provided by what happened in Bohemia and Moravia (in the Austrian half of the Empire) and Slovakia (in the Hungarian half). Among both the Czechs in Bohemia and Moravia and among the Slovaks in Slovakia the sense of nationhood became increasingly powerful during the last decades of the nineteenth century. And in both cases, the actions of the state and the development of the economy were important contributing factors. In Bohemia and Moravia, industrialization and commercial development in this the most economically advanced parts of the Habsburg lands, brought Czechs into the towns, into commercial occupations and spawned a growing Czech bourgeoisie. However, the German population was ill-disposed to give up its privileged position, and German remained the official language in the schools, universities, government offices and the courts. Ambitious Czechs were faced with the choice either of adapting themselves to German or else to protest, and increasing numbers opted for the latter. In Slovakia, the battle lines were harder: there the Magyar ruling class pursued a harsh policy of cultural assimilation which left little room for the Slovak language or Slovak culture.

The case of the Czechs and the Slovaks suggests that the activities of the state – determining what language would be used in education and in government – and economic development (particularly among the more prosperous Czechs) played an important role in formenting nationalist feeling. By abandoning the old principle of dynastic allegiance as the cement which held the monarchy together, and opening the gates to more modern consideration of 'national' concerns – maintaining the privileges of some nationalities *as nationalities* over the interests of others – the Dual Monarchy sowed the seeds of its eventual undoing.

France

Now, let us turn our gaze to the other end of the spectrum, to the classic example of the centralized unitary state (and one which existed in coherent and recognizable form throughout the nineteenth century): France. It might be argued that German national identity owed much to (Prussian) state-propelled nation-building – which came to define what it meant to be 'German' – that Polish national identity took shape in struggles against states which administered lands inhabited by Poles, and that Italian national identity owed much to a unification which spread from the kingdom of Piedmont in the north west. In the case of France, however, the formation of French national identity in the nineteenth century must have had other origins. After all, there had been a 'France' in the eighteenth century, and the French state had a long tradition of centralized administration and control. Does this mean that the processes of nation-building, and of the role of state and economy in these processes, were fundamentally different? Or can we apply the same sorts of generalizations to the French case as elsewhere?

In order to provide you with some materials with which to frame answers to these questions, two chapters of what Anderson (p.153) refers to as 'the best study ever made of social and economic modernization in any European country', of Eugen Weber's *Peasants into Frenchmen. The Modernization of Rural France, 1870–1914*, (Chapter Seven, 'France, One and Indivisible', pp.95–114; and Chapter Twenty-nine, 'Cultures and Civilizations', pp.485–96) have been included in the Offprints Collection as Offprint 11. Weber's general thesis, that it was not until the late nineteenth century that rural France (i.e. the bulk of the country) 'was integrated into the modern world and the official culture – of Paris, of the cities', has provoked considerable discussion.

According to Weber (on the opening page of Offprint 11(B)): 'The modern view of the nation as a body of people united according to their own will and having certain attributes in common (not least history) was at best dubiously applicable to the France of 1870.' Doubts have been raised about Weber's thesis – about 'the dubious modernization model on which his argument is based' (Magraw, 1983, p.321), about whether the transition from traditional to 'modern' French society was so smooth and unilinear as Weber suggests, or about whether rural France really was as isolated as Weber (who draws his examples largely from inland Brittany, the central Massif and the Pyrenees, and largely ignores 'core' regions) paints it. For the moment, at least, assume that Weber is right, and that the decisive shifts in mentalities which turned 'peasants' into 'Frenchmen' occurred during the years 1870 to 1914.

Exercise   You should now read Offprint 11 (A) and (B). What do you think may have been the key developments in the economy and the state which contributed to the decisive shifts in mentalities which turned 'peasants' into 'Frenchmen' during the years 1870 to 1914?

Discussion The factors which I would highlight are the development of a (national) railway network, linking the various regions of the country and linking rural areas to the towns and the national capital; the spread of public schooling, in which children were taught the *national* language; the importance of military conscription, which brought men (just as they came of age) from all regions of the country together in a single 'school of the nation'; and the development and spread of national newspapers, which were written in the national language. All these developments are discussed at length by Weber in his book, and all figure in Anderson's text as well.

Another extremely important insight to be gained from Weber's work concerns the extent to which the creation of the French 'nation' in the nineteenth century can be viewed as a successful campaign of colonial conquest. Note, for example, what Weber has to say, towards the end of Offprint 11(A), about 'cultural imperialism' and 'attempts to impose a "dominant civilization on a composite society"' and his suggestion that this may describe not only Pan-German or Pan-Slav movements and European colonial expansion (as in Algeria), but could apply to France itself as well. This indeed is a theme which lurks behind much of nineteenth-century European history: the expansion of metropolitan European power and of its 'civilization'. This, as Weber suggests, was not limited to the crusade to civilize the 'savages' in Africa and/or Asia; it also involved parallel campaigns at 'home', in France. (Weber's first chapter is entitled 'a country of savages', and he is referring to France. He begins his text by quoting from Balzac, speaking of the Burgundian countryside in his *Paysans* (1844): 'You don't need to go to America to see savages. Here are the Redskins of Fenimore Cooper' (Weber, 1976, p.3).) The creation of a 'nation' meant the 'civilizing' of the – 'savages' – whether in Algeria, Cameroon, Siberia, or Burgundy.

Weber's work casts doubts upon the idea that a unitary state structure necessarily creates a unitary national identity. Yes, one might assert that it did so eventually; by 1914 Weber's peasants had become 'Frenchmen' (who signed up in their millions to defend their 'patrie' against the invading Germans, even if many had never before been to northern France where the war was fought, and who displayed a spirit quite different from the widespread indifference which had accompanied the declaration of war against Prussia in 1870). Yet, what conclusions can we draw about the effectiveness of the (unitary, French) state in forging a nation before 1870? If Weber is right, it certainly had been limited, perhaps by the fact that so many inhabitants of rural France still were living a subsistence existence, largely unconnected to national markets or economies – a conclusion which suggests that economic development may ultimately have formed the driving force behind the creation of 'nations' in the nineteenth century. (This is a theme to which we shall return below in the section entitled 'Economy and nation', p.120.)

Yet counter-arguments can be made. To begin with, one may question whether all the decisive shifts occurred during the period after the Franco-Prussian War. There was considerable internal migration within France even by 1870, and massive military mobilizations before the creation of the

Third Republic; and cultural habits had developed across France before 1870 which arguably served to make people 'French'. (Think of Robert Tombs's discussion on Video 3 of the importance of having babies – or not, as often was the case in France throughout the nineteenth century.) Perhaps most importantly, there was, unquestionably, a unitary French state with an élite national political culture in the first half of the nineteenth century. To emphasize the post-1870 period tends to give economic development a rather superior role to that of state action in promoting national consciousness, which raises the question: Does not an emphasis on the post-1870 period, by focusing on economic developments and the consequent spread of popular cultural norms, perhaps underplay the importance of that unitary state and imply a particular norm which itself is a nationalist ideal? By assuming that Weber's approach is the correct one, we may run the risk of essentially defining 'nations' and national consciousness as nationalists define them and then using that definition as a guide when tracing the creation of the 'nation', rather than looking critically at nationalist assumptions and at what really is central to nation-state formation and viability.

State and nation

Beginning the final paragraph of Chapter 4 ('States and Nations'), Anderson asserts: 'Nationalism has shown itself during the last century or more the only force capable of involving the ordinary man [sic!] deeply and personally with the state of which he [sic!] is a member' (p.250). Is he right? What exactly did this 'nationalism' consist of? And what caused it to coalesce and to develop such potency? One way of approaching these questions is to consider the possibility that much of the story of nationalism in nineteenth-century Europe might be read as the reverse of what Anderson suggests: namely that nationalism is, to some extent at least, the product of structures and actions of European states (whether dynastic or republican), rather than the main force which served to buttress states in their relationship with their subjects, that is that states underpin nationalism rather than that nationalism underpins states.

Such a conclusion may be something of an overstatement, but keep it at least as a working hypothesis as you begin to examine the connections between state and nation. To a considerable degree, the interconnections of 'state' and nation creation already have been outlined in previous units of this block, in particular the materials on language and education (Unit 13) and on 'oppression, domination and integration' (Unit 12). (Such considerations should not be altogether absent from discussion of culture and religion in nineteenth-century Europe either: particularly within states where there has been a state Church and where national identity became bound up with identification with a particular (state) religion. Perhaps the most striking example of this was Tsarist Russia, where Russian identity was closely bound up with Russian Orthodoxy and 'Holy Russia'.) Now, however, we need to make some of the possible links and questions about them more explicit.

Exercise   Now that you have worked through the first four units of Block 3 and the introductory section of this unit, you ought to be in a position to draw provisional conclusions about contributions of the state to building the 'nation' in nineteenth-century Europe. How do you think the state interventions changed people's lives in nineteenth-century Europe and, thereby, affected ways in which they viewed themselves in terms of national identity?

Discussion   Rather than present my own thoughts in answer to this question, I shall offer some observations by Eric Hobsbawm (1992), from his recent enquiry into *Nations and Nationalism since 1780* (a stimulating text on nationalism, and one which you should consider reading in its entirety): state interventions

> In the course of the nineteenth century these interventions became so universal and so routinized in 'modern' states that a family would have to live in some very inaccessible place if some member or other were not to come into regular contact with the national state and its agents: through the postman, the policeman or gendarme, and eventually through the schoolteacher; through the men employed on the railways, where these were publicly owned; not to mention the garrisons of soldiers and the even more widely available military bands. Increasingly the state kept records of each of its subjects and citizens through the device of regular periodic censuses (which did not become general until the middle of the nineteenth century), through theoretically compulsory attendance at primary school and, where applicable, military conscription. In bureaucratic and well-policed states a system of personal documentation and registration brought the inhabitant into even more direct contact with the machinery of rule and administration, especially if he or she moved from one place to another. In states which provided a civil alternative to the ecclesiastical celebration of the great human rites, as most did, inhabitants might encounter the representatives of the state on these emotionally charged occasions; and always they would be recorded by the machinery for registering births, marriages and deaths, which supplemented the machinery of censuses. Government and subject or citizen were inevitably linked by daily bonds, as never before. And nineteenth-century revolutions in transport and communications typified by the railway and the telegraph tightened and routinized the links between central authority and its remotest outposts. (Hobsbawm, 1992, pp.80–1)

This strikes me both as a fine outline of the main relevant points, and a good description of the development of the world in which we live today – in which we expect to find ourselves educated, policed, conscripted, counted, registered and taxed by the bureaucratic governmental machinery of a nation-state.

Now let us pick up some of the main points which Hobsbawm mentions. The first is the spread of state education, which in north-western Europe developed into systems of compulsory mass primary education, with an army of salaried teachers, which succeeded in establishing virtually universal literacy (in national languages!) in the late nineteenth century – one of the great social revolutions of recent history. You already have examined in some detail the extension of state education in Unit 13 – a theme to which Anderson attaches great importance. On p.215 he asserts forcefully: 'The growth of universal, or at least large-scale, primary education went during the century in step with the growth of popular nationalism: the second hardly could have existed without the first'. A point to remember here is that this 'large-scale, primary education' was organized and delivered by the state. If Anderson is right about the relationship of the growth of primary education and the growth of popular nationalism (of a sense of national identity), then this is a crucial area where the state has been instrumental in constructing the nation.

The extension of education delivered more than just literacy. The new curriculum often was also a national one; it aimed to deliver respect for the 'fatherland', a sense of nationhood. In rural France in the 1870s schoolchildren were taught, and repeated back to their teachers, that 'the fatherland is both your village, your province, it is all of France. The fatherland is like a great family' (quoted in Weber, 1976, p.333). Throughout newly united Germany, in Baden no less than in Prussia, in Jewish and Catholic *Gymnasien* no less than in Protestant ones, pupils ritually celebrated the birthday of 'His Majesty our Kaiser'. (*Jahresberichte* of various *Gymnasien* and *Realschulen* between 1871 and 1900.) State schools became schools of the nation.

Another key point raised by Hobsbawm concerns the armed forces and conscription. This forms the sharp end of the state's relationship with its citizens/subjects; and there has been a long history of popular antipathy against the military, in nineteenth-century Europe, particularly in the countryside. The armed forces often were regarded as an army of occupation in their own country: they gobbled up food and taxes, and they took away sons who were needed at home – a particularly serious matter in the countryside where a son's labour was required on the family farm. What is more, arbitrary systems of conscription – whereby the better off often could buy their way out of military service – and the domination of the officer corps by the nobility, served to reinforce popular hostility towards the army. However, something important in the nature of European armed forces changed in the course of the nineteenth century: armies began to become armies of the nation rather simply armies of the state. Eugen Weber describes this process in France – a process which provided reinforcement for his 'peasants into Frenchmen' thesis – particularly well. Until the final decades of the century (in the wake of the Franco-Prussian War and, then, the abolition in 1889 of the lottery system which hitherto had governed conscription and its replacement by a system which effectively delivered universal conscription), there had been 'little sense of national identity to mitigate the hostility and fear most country people felt for troops' (Weber, 1976, p.297):

It is likely that the war with Prussia, which mobilized unusually great numbers while focusing attention on their fate, a war also in which the connection between local and national interests became more evident to large numbers of people, marked the beginning of the change. The old prejudices took time to die, and the 1870s offer scattered instances of enduring antipathy. But the role played by the war in promoting national awareness was reinforced by educational propaganda, by developing trade and commercial ties, and finally by something approaching universal service. By the 1890s there is persuasive evidence that the army was no longer 'theirs' but 'ours'. Ill-feelings between troops and civilians were countered by the sense of nationality being learned in the school, and in the barracks too. At least for a while, the army could become what its enthusiasts hoped for: the school of the fatherland. (Weber, 1976, p.298)

As the 'school of the fatherland' or school of the nation, national armies formed a key aspect of the state's role in creating 'nations' in nineteenth-century Europe.

A third key area, which Hobsbawm mentions, is regulation by state organizations. Increasingly during the course of the nineteenth century, Europeans came to be regulated by the state, within national boundaries. They were counted by states in national censuses, and their births and deaths were recorded by the state rather than by the Church. Comprehensive national legal codes were developed which regulated both commercial affairs and, increasingly, people's everyday lives. (The link between unified legal codes and nation was perhaps clearest in nineteenth-century Germany, where, as Michael John (1989) has pointed out, 'the campaign for a national legal system was a prominent feature of political debate'; there the first great national code, the Commercial Code *(Handelsgesetzbuch)* was completed in 1861, and the Civil Code *(Bürgerliches Gesetzbuch)* was produced within the context of the unified Reich and concluded in 1896.) The prices which people paid for their food and other items were affected by national tariff barriers which were erected by states to protect national industries. Increasingly, the day-to-day activities of Europeans meant that they regularly came into contact with, and had their daily activities regulated by, the apparatuses of the state. Increasingly, the state defined how people lived and who people were, and thus defined the 'nation'.

Economy and nation

To what extent is national identity determined by economic development? Obviously, economic developments are important: (national?) labour markets, (national?) currencies, (national?) taxation, and (national?) commercial markets, supply reference points for much of people's lives. It is equally obvious that the ways in which these developments structure people's everyday lives – where one searches for and finds work, where one spends the money in one's pocket, where one pays taxes – help frame a sense of national identity. In all these areas, Europeans experienced revolutionary changes in the course of the nineteenth century. We now need to consider rather more closely how these processes developed in Europe during the nineteenth century, and look at what their connections might have been to the 'creation of the nation'.

Exercise   Before we proceed to consider these economic developments systematically, however, let us examine a general thesis about how economics may have framed (a particular) national identity: that propounded by Harold James in a recent book which he entitled *A German Identity*. Please now read Offprint 12. How would you characterize James's argument?

Discussion   Perhaps the best way to answer this question is to highlight how James himself outlines his general thesis. In his 'Introduction', he wrote:

> My argument is concerned with the emergence in the mid-nineteenth century of a doctrine of nationality that justified the existence of the nation primarily by reference to the inexorable logic of economic development. Such a view took the place previously occupied by theories emphasizing cultural identities. Instead of being a cultural community, or a political unit based on a shared culture, the nation became the framework for an economic process that would in turn create political and cultural consciousness. (James, 1989, p.3)

The question then is, why? In the chapter you have read (Offprint 12), at the beginning of the section on 'Realpolitik and Determinism', James puts the question thus: 'Why did railways matter more than romanticism, and tariffs more than tales of the Fatherland?' His answer is that 'this change was a consequence of the collapse of the hopes of 1848', which resulted in a 're-evaluation of the course of German history': 'It was no longer a story of national awakening, but rather a more sober tale of institutional arrangements designed to promote prosperity.' The point here is that people in the German states increasingly looked to economics as the basis for nationhood. This was reflected in 'an economic determinism of the type that became commonplace to German thinkers after the middle of the century' – the context in which James places the work of Karl Marx. James's story of German nationalism in the nineteenth century is a story of the triumph of 'economic determinism', which finally was embodied in the 'materialism of the new Reich' of 1870/1.

Is James right? Did tariffs really matter more than tales of the Fatherland, and if so, how are we to measure this? And is it really possible to separate out the economic components of a nationalist movement? As can be seen from much of the material assembled for this unit, it is difficult to isolate the cultural, economic and political components of nationalist movements. James's assertion that 'instead of being a cultural community, or a political unit based on a shared culture, the nation became the framework for an economic process that would in turn create political and cultural consciousness', is thus a matter for debate, not a statement of fact. (It is, however, perhaps not so surprising that this thesis is put forward by an economic historian, whose most important work has been on the political economy of twentieth-century Germany.)

(Note that the great eclectic architectural expressions of the 'materialism of the new Reich', the great 'national' buildings mentioned by James which were constructed in Berlin after unification (the Reichstag, the Cathedral), are shown and discussed in TV3, 'A Question of Identity: Berlin and Berliners'.)

If, as James asserts, it is indeed 'the inexorable logic of economic development' which 'justified the existence of the nation', more consideration needs to be given to economic developments which may form a 'nation' and link it together. Nineteenth-century Europe saw the development of national markets, national currencies, and – to return to that subject dear to the heart of Friedrich List – national railway networks. The nineteenth century was the century of railway building, and the railway networks built were 'national' in that they tended to link the provinces with the 'national' capital (Paris, London, Berlin, Brussels, St Petersburg) and to link not only industrial centres and smaller towns but also, with the building of branch lines, rural regions with a national market.

National markets require national currencies. As any observer of the heated debates in Britain about a single European currency during the past few years can testify, money has a real and symbolic value which is about more than just economics. It also involves sovereignty and with this, national identity; if economics can form national identity, then one of its clearest expressions is a national currency. A currency, and a decision to establish a single national currency, thus lies at the intersection of state, economy and nation. The importance of a currency in the creation of a nation was perhaps best illustrated by the case of Germany. During the first two-thirds of the nineteenth century, what was to become 'Germany' saw the circulation of different currencies and different sets of weights and measures. Even though the creation of the *Zollverein* ('Customs Union') of 1834 did away with so many customs barriers between German states, they continued to use different currencies. This created considerable difficulties for trade across the boundaries of the various German states – and, by extension, placed obstacles before the creation of a unified German 'nation'. Various banks in the various states which later formed the Reich had the right to issue bank notes, although the vast majority of the currency in circulation in the German states were Thalers issued by the Preussische Bank (the 'Prussian Bank' as the Prussian state-owned Königliche Bank – 'Royal Bank' – became in 1846, and which in 1865 began to establish branches outside Prussia) (Born, 1983, pp.12–13). Monetary unification was a consequence of political unification, a realization of demands by German liberals within the framework of a conservative federal state: In 1871 the Thaler was replaced by the Mark, and in 1875 the Reichsbank was established (emerging from the Preussische Bank, which was sold to the Reich), and uniform regulations regarding the issuing of bank notes were passed. Although other banks retained their right to issue notes, many suspended note issue soon after the establishment of the Reichsbank; and although the Bayerische Notenbank in Bavaria, the Sächsische Bank in Saxony, the Badische Bank in Baden and the Württembergische Notenbank in Württemberg still were issuing notes on the eve of the First World War, Reichsbank notes were accepted throughout the Empire and unified Germany in effect came to possess a unified currency.

In many ways, the development of a German currency seems to confirm the general argument put forward by Harold James: that, in contradistinction to the nationalist rhetoric of Herder and Fichte, who saw education and culture as the basis of German national identity, it was economics which really provided the framework for German national identity in the nineteenth century. 'Germany' came to be conceived of as an economic entity (i.e. in terms of what it could deliver in a material sense) rather than in cultural terms. And there is no more real representation of that economic entity than money.

Before moving on from this section on economy and nation, however, let us examine the interplay of economic links and nationality in an industrial region which straddled political frontiers and ethnic boundaries: Upper Silesia. The Upper Silesian mineral basin is the European continent's oldest heavy-industrial region; it was there, in Tarnowitz in 1792, that the first coke blast furnace on the European continent came into operation. Whereas the mineral basin, with its deposits of coal, iron and zinc, was a geological unity, throughout the nineteenth century it was divided politically between Prussia/Germany and the Russian Empire. It also was divided ethnically and linguistically between Poles and Germans. The ethnic divisions did not neatly parallel the political frontiers, however; linguistically and ethnically mixed populations straddled the borders. In Prussian Upper Silesia, for example, a large proportion of the industrial work-force, especially in the mines, was Polish, and the countryside was overwhelmingly Polish speaking, while ownership of the industrial enterprises and the state administration remained in German hands.

Although the lion's share of the region's natural resources were to be found in the Prussian Province of Silesia, the political division had important consequences for Upper Silesia's economic development. Most importantly, it placed barriers – border controls – between the movement of labour (particularly from the less developed and more rural districts in the Russian Empire to the more industrialized Prussian towns). This was particularly true during the last two decades of the nineteenth century, when the growth of industry created a huge demand for labour. In 1885 the Prussian government, concerned about the ethnic mix along the eastern frontiers, closed the border and began to expel non-Prussian Poles (i.e. Poles from the Russian and Habsburg Empires). Also, the main markets for the Upper Silesian coal and iron and steel industries were domestic, that is 'German'; Upper Silesian coal was sold in the Austro-Hungarian Empire and in Russian Poland, but access to the latter market was limited by restrictive tariffs which were a consequence of deteriorating German-Russian relations from the mid-1870s. Furthermore, it may be noted in this context, the state played an extremely important direct role in Upper Silesian heavy industry until 1865: for example, the Prussian state played the key role in hiring and firing miners in Upper Silesia, despite formally private ownership of the mines.

So, Upper Silesians on the Prussian side of the border were linked into the Prussian/German economy and Prussian/German labour market, and administered by the Prussian/German state. What are we to make of this? Did the interventions of the (Prussian) state and economic links create a sense of 'nation'? Obviously not, for the ethnic divisions remained, and even became stronger, in the course of the nineteenth century. Polish nationalism in Upper Silesia was not diluted by the fact the Prussian Poles worked for German companies in a German labour market, learned the German language and went to German schools. Indeed, after the First World War the ethnic divisions were to explode into violence in formerly Prussian Upper Silesia, in the form of three Polish risings against German rule. Here state and culture appear to have been more important in 'the creation of the nation' and national consciousness than economy.

Groups outside 'nations'

I want to close this unit by considering two groups which   not easily fit
into the discussion of 'state and economy in the creation of the nation' as it
has been structured thus far. The such first group to be considered is one
which played an exceedingly important role in the history of modern
Europe but which does not fit easily into discussions of nation-building:
Europe's Jews. (Jews have surfaced rather little in A221 thus far, but Norman Davies discusses the Jews in Poland and Zionism in Video 3.) Jews are
given very little space in the text by Anderson, mentioned only on pp.221–
4 (and then largely in the context of discussing anti-Semitism). Yet their
history is an integral part of the history of nineteenth-century Europe. In
the course of the nineteenth century Europe's Jews were, at different times
and to differing degrees, emancipated from legal restrictions on how they
might earn their livings and where they might reside. From France and
Germany to Bohemia and Congress Poland (after 1862) Jews increasingly
looked at assimilation as the way forward. In Congress Poland, there were
signs of a turn away from Yiddish (at least among the better-off) as the language of the ghetto and concerted attempts to speak Polish. Then came
1881 – the year of the great pogroms in the Russian Empire proper and in
Warsaw (which contained the largest Jewish community in Poland). Not
only did the change in climate spark large-scale migration westward (especially to the United States and, to a lesser extent, to Britain); during the
last decades of the nineteenth century, eastern European Jews – increasingly urbanized and faced with growing hostility and anti-Semitism – came
to regard themselves (unlike their western European co-religionists) more
in national terms. These years saw a renaissance of the Yiddish language,
and, politically, eastern European Jews turned increasingly towards either
socialism or Zionism – the movement to establish a Jewish homeland in
Palestine, a 'nationalist answer to a nationalist challenge' (Haumann,
1990, p.149).

   Of course, the main appeal of Zionism was amongst poorer Jews
under the jurisdiction of the Russian Empire, that is amongst people subject to discrimination on national grounds. In western Europe, the great
bulk of Jews wanted to integrate into the nation-states in which they lived
(i.e. become British, French, German, etc.). And even in eastern Europe
the preferred alternative to assimilation into their state of birth was not to
seek a new life in Jewish homeland of Palestine but rather to emigrate to
the United States. Nevertheless, it is worth reflecting on the aspirations of
the Zionist movement, which were very much an expression of European
political culture in the late nineteenth century: to achieve a *national* state
and homeland for the Jews, who thus would become like a normal European 'nation'. That the aspirations of Zionist Jews came to resemble the
aspirations of other ('national') groups is testimony to the force of
nationalism and of the perceived link between state and nation which
developed in nineteenth-century Europe. Whether it was true or not, the
achievement of the nation-state came to be regarded as the self-evident confirmation of the progress of an ethnic, cultural or linguistic group. No less
than Mazzini, with his call 'every nation a state', Theodor Herzl, the
author of *Der Judenstaat* ('The Jewish State') and father of modern Zion-

ism, was a product of his time and place, of late nineteenth-century central Europe. No doubt Herzl would have agreed with the socialist Karl Renner (like Herzl, a subject of the multi-national Habsburg Empire), who wrote in 1899:

> Once a certain degree of European development has been reached, the linguistic and cultural communities of peoples, having silently matured throughout the centuries, emerge from the world of passive existence as peoples. They become conscious of themselves as a force with a historical destiny. They demand control over the state, as the highest available instrument of power, and strive for their self-determination. (Karl Renner, *Staat und Nation*, Vienna, 1899, p.89; quoted in Hobsbawm, 1992, p.101)

In his survey of *Nations and Nationalism since 1870*, Eric Hobsbawm has described Renner's statement as an exercise in 'programmatic mythology'. Perhaps 'mythology', rather than 'state and economy', ultimately is what 'the creation of the nation', in Europe of the nineteenth century (and of today), really has been about.

The second group, if that is the right term, that I would like to mention in closing is women. It seems striking, to me at least, that women have not figured in the discussion of 'nation' at all thus far. You may remember that, at the beginning of section on 'State and nation' (p.117), I noted in passing Anderson's seemingly unreflected use of 'man' when emphasizing the power of nationalism (in the final paragraph of Chapter 4 ('States and Nations') of Anderson: 'Nationalism has show itself during the last century or more the only force capable of involving the ordinary man [sic!] deeply and personally with the state of which he [sic!] is a member' (p.250)). Perhaps – and I have no way of knowing for certain – this assessment gives Anderson insufficient credit; maybe he chose his words quite consciously and deliberately. Might not such a statement rightly reflect that most of the themes discussed in this unit – the links between state interventions and economic developments on the one hand and the 'creation of the nation' on the other – concern the lives of European *men* much more than those of European *women*? Conscription obviously was an exclusively male affair; involvement in political life (whether in government, political parties, or at the polling booth) was something from which women were almost completely excluded; the police, and most of the people against whom they directed their attentions, were male; economic life tended to be dominated by men. The sort of things which we have tended to regard as nation-building are also facets of public life in which men dominate. Women figure very little in the story of European nationalism and nation-building in the nineteenth century. (With the exceptions of Joan of Arc and the Virgin Mary, women appear hardly at all in Eric Hobsbawn's *Nations and Nationalism since 1780*.) That may not be an oversight, but rather an accurate representation of the theme of this unit.

This point has been noted by Lucy Riall (1994), in her excellent survey of the Italian Risorgimento. Discussing the intense sense of disappointment which followed the Italian unification in the 1860s, Riall emphasizes not only the regional and class divides in Italians' attitudes towards the Italian nation-state – that 'the members of the middle-class circles who read nationalist newspapers and participated in National Society debates in Northern and Central Italy cared little, if at all, for the demands of

Sicilian peasants' but also that the 'new, public sphere' in which consciousness of national identity developed 'excluded all but the most wealthy and literate' and that 'as such, national identity was defined very narrowly. Not only the poor and illiterate but all women [...] were excluded from legitimate participation in this new national public sphere' (Riall, 1994, pp.74–5).

These observations point to an aspect of 'the creation of the nation' which should not be overlooked: namely that the 'nationalization of the masses' in nineteenth-century Europe referred largely to male subjects (see Mosse, 1991). Women were largely excluded from the processes involved in this 'nationalization' – most obviously, from national conscripted armies, but also as taxpayers and, of course, as voters. As nation-states developed in nineteenth-century Europe, they increasingly defined who was included and who was excluded from the 'nation'. Unlike the dynastic state, the state which identified with one nationality in effect defined that nationality by political participation, by participation in the public sphere (and increasingly by voting). It was precisely this sort of participation from which women were largely excluded in nineteenth-century Europe, indeed until the First World War. It is not really until the twentieth century that one could speak with confidence in Europe about the nationalization of women as well as men, about the inclusion of women as well as men into the national community and allowing women to be full citizens of the nation-state. For nineteenth-century Europe, however, nationalism probably needs to be understood as a man's game.

References

Born, K. E. (1983), *International Banking in the 19th and 20th Centuries*, Berg Publishers, Leamington Spa.

Davies, N. (1982), *God's Playground. A History of Poland. Volume II: 1795 to the Present*, Oxford University Press, Oxford.

Eley, G. (1986), 'German politics and Polish nationalists: The dialectic of nation forming in the east of Prussia', in *From Unification to Nazism. Reinterpreting the German Past*, Allen and Unwin, London.

Gildea, R. (1987), *Barricades and Borders. Europe 1800–1914*, Oxford University Press, Oxford.

Hagen, W. W. (1980), *Germans, Poles, and Jews. The Nationality Conflict in the Prussian East, 1772–1914*, Chicago University Press, Chicago and London.

Haumann, H. (1990), *Geschichte der Ostjuden*, Deutscher Taschenburch, Verlag, Munich.

Hobsbawm, E. J. (1992), *Nations and Nationalism since 1870. Programme, Myth, Reality*, 2nd edn, Cambridge University Press, Cambridge.

James, H. (1989), *A German Identity 1770–1990*, Weidenfeld and Nicholson, London.

John, M. (1980), *Politics and the Law in Late Nineteenth-Century Germany. The Origins of the Legal Code*, Oxford University Press, Oxford.

Lyttleton, A. (1993), 'The national question in Italy', in M. Teich and R. Porter (eds), *The National Question in Europe in Historical Context*, Cambridge University Press, Cambridge.

Magraw, R. (1983), *France 1815–1914. The Bourgeois Century*, Fontana, London.

Mosse, G. (1991), *The Nationalization of the Masses: Political Symbolism and Mass Movements in Germany from the Napoleonic Wars through the Third Reich*, Cornell University Press, Ithica, New York, and London.

Pounds, N.J.G. (1985), *An Historical Geography of Europe 1880–1914*, Cambridge University Press, Cambridge.

Riall, L. (1994), *The Italian Risorgimento. State, Society and National Unification* Routledge, London.

Ritter, G. A. (1980), *Wahlgeschichtliches Arbeitsbuch. Materialien zur Statistik des Kaiserreichs 1871–1918*, C. H. Beck, Munich.

Treue, W. (1979), *Gesellschaft, Wirtschaft under Technik Deutschlands im 19. Jahrhundert*, Deutscher Taschenbuch Verlag, Munich.

Weber, E. (1976), *Peasants into Frenchmen. The Modernization of Rural France, 1870–1914*, Stanford University Press, Stanford.

Unit 16
Conclusion: the making of modern Europe?

Prepared for the course team by Richard Bessel

Contents

Study timetable

Weeks of study	Text	Video	AC
2	Unit 16; Anderson	Video 3	

From the nineteenth century to the twentieth

Shortly before he died in 1990, Tim Mason (one of the foremost historians of twentieth-century Germany) wrote:

> All good history writing begins at the end. However artfully it may be disguised, however unthinkingly it may be assumed, the end of the story is there at the beginning. Where the end is judged to lie in time, what its character is, how it is defined – in taking these decisions about any piece of work, historians necessarily make their judgement about the general significance of their particular theme or period. And this judgement in turn determines where they start. (Mason, 1993, p.1)

When making these comments, Mason was wrestling with his own attempts to make sense of the history of the 'Third Reich'. However, the validity of this observation is not limited to that tortured history. Indeed, it provides an apt description of the way in which historians of all periods and countries work, whether consciously or not. It is no less valid for efforts to make sense of the history of nineteenth-century Europe than for attempts to struggle with the history of Nazi Germany. A history of nineteenth-century Europe which seeks to explain why it ended in the disaster of the First World War obviously will look very different from a history which seeks to explain why most of the world's developed industrial economies were European when the nineteenth century drew to a close. In A221, your work has been organized around three key themes – state, economy, nation – and implicit in each of these are different 'ends'. In these final comments, I would like to offer a few thoughts about the 'ends' of the histories of nineteenth-century Europe which you have studied over the past months, and to discuss at least one important aspect of the relationship of nineteenth-century Europe, which you have studied, to twentieth-century Europe, in which you have lived. I hope that this might provide an interesting, as well as helpful, aid in looking back over the course as a whole.

In a recent essay John Breuilly, who served as External Assessor for A221, has observed:

> Historians seek to understand change over time. They cannot wipe from their minds their knowledge of how more recent history relates to more distant history. Nor should they, even if they could, because it would involve tossing away the one advantage the historian enjoys over the historical actors – that is, knowing what comes next. (Breuilly, 1992, pp.278–9)

This is not a plea to subscribe to a teleological approach towards historical study – to assume that the way things ended was the way they had to end and, consequently, to include discussion of those developments which can be seen to have led to that particular end and to dismiss or ignore those developments which do not appear as steps in a march towards the perceived end. Nor is it to suggest that there really is only one 'end'. In fact, it is the opposite: it is to underscore the importance of choosing which 'end' one is writing towards and attempting to explain. After all, we possess many different visions of 'what comes next'.

Let me offer an example from A221: One can, as Ian Donnachie does in Unit 8, quite legitimately write about 'the transformation of agriculture' in nineteenth-century Europe, taking as a central theme the development of a world market in agricultural produce (with the advances in transport technology and the opening up of vast agricultural lands in North and South America). The 'end' of the political side of that story involves the rise of protectionism as a reaction 'to the blast of overseas competition'. Or one could perhaps concentrate more on the persistence of subsistence agriculture, of agricultural economies which differed little from those of the Middle Ages (think back to what Paul Preston said about nineteenth-century Spain in Video 3), across large swathes of the European continent and on the very backward rural communities which supplied so much of the manpower for the slaughter of 1914–18 and support in the Russian countryside after 1917 for a revolutionary regime which appeared to guarantee the removal of the landowning class. On the opening page of the 'Introduction' to the set book (p.ix), Anderson notes that 'During the eighteenth century the continent was still, in its everyday life, closer to the twelfth century than to the twentieth'. Of course, this judgement depends a great deal on one's picture of the twentieth century, but it would not be misleading to note that, at the beginning of the twentieth century large parts of Europe from Andalucia in southern Spain to villages on the Russian steppe were still, in their everyday life, 'closer to the twelfth century than to the twentieth'.

So, to apply the observation by Tim Mason about 'ends and beginnings' to the subject of A221 as a whole: Where did the nineteenth century end, and where did the twentieth century begin? Did the nineteenth century end on the Marne in 1914, when the German invasion of France got bogged down and the four-year-long 'Great War' of attrition began which undermined Europe's position at the forefront of the world's economy, led to the destruction of the German, Austro-Hungarian and Russian monarchies and fundamentally altered the political map of the continent? Did the nineteenth century end at the Winter Palace in Petrograd in 1917, when the Old Order disintegrated in the face of popular rebellion and Leninist determination? If the nineteenth century is regarded as coterminous with 'the ascendancy of Europe', then does it end with the eclipse of European (and British) power (economic and political) by that of the United States during the First World War? There is no single 'right' answer here; the ways in which we might respond are indicative of the ways in which we regard and organize the history of nineteenth-century Europe.

You will remember that we (Clive Emsley and I) begin the Introduction to this course with Thomas Nipperdey's arresting opening statement in the first of his three-volume history of nineteenth-century Germany: 'In the beginning was Napoleon'. That was intended to get you to think about how we organize historical study, in this case of nineteenth-century Europe. Nipperdey's statement indicates one path, among many, to approach the history of nineteenth-century Europe. And, as you worked through this course, you may have concluded that it is an apposite way to begin such a history. The French Wars, and Napoleon's conquests, were fundamental in giving rise to new state structures, new government bureaucracies, new national identities (in reaction to the French). But it is, of course, not the only way to begin. We could have started with industrialization, putting economic development at the forefront of our enquiry; or we could have started with population growth, Europe's striking demographic development at the centre of our investigation of the nineteenth century. You now should be in a position to make some judgements for yourself about where best to begin. But, following from what Tim Mason wrote, that is also a question of where you see the end to be.

The purpose of this short concluding unit is to help you put the Course as a whole into perspective – not just to re-enforce the materials about particular themes (be they policing, industrialization, education or whatever), but also to link these themes together. This is not designed to be a review of the course; the best way to review the course is to re-read those parts of it which you found particularly interesting, enlightening or useful, not to wade through more material which essentially repeats what you already have done. Rather, this is a short essay designed to offer some general points about the themes of the course as a whole and to raise the question of how the history of Europe in the nineteenth century relates to the history of Europe in the twentieth.

Each of the three main themes around which A221 has been organized – state, economy, nation – both delineate key developments which unfolded in nineteenth-century Europe and point ahead to developments in the twentieth. The modern state, which took shape in the nineteenth century as state functions expanded with (among other things) the growth of educational provision and the beginnings of comprehensive social insurance, developed in twentieth-century Europe into formations which at times regulated virtually all aspects of social and economic life, consumed the lion's share of economic activity in many countries, and became the largest employer and provider of goods and services. It also developed into the totalitarian nightmares of Nazi Germany and Stalinist Russia, both of which had mutated from the bureaucratic states and utopian dreams of the nineteenth century. The modern economy, which took shape in the nineteenth century as European regions industrialized (albeit at different times and at different rates) and as modern economic cycles of growth and recession began to determine the living conditions of millions of people, buffeted the inhabitants of twentieth-century Europe with a violence previously unimaginable as the 'Great Depression' which began in 1873 was put into the shade by the 'Great Depression' which began in 1929 and the great boom which preceded the First World War was vastly overshadowed by the great boom which followed the Second. And modern nationalism, which was a child of nineteenth-century Europe, threatened to rip apart the Europe of the twentieth – perhaps nowhere more so than in the Balkans, where the break-up of the Ottoman and Habsburg empires and the upsurge in national feeling led to bitter conflict which has persisted for the whole of the twentieth century. Indeed it may be that Europe's twentieth century will end in the same place as did Europe's nineteenth century: in Sarajevo. Of course, none of these sets of developments necessarily can be described as if they formed a consistent trend or process; the 'growth of the state', for example, was in some respects reversed after 1945 as the balance of public and private power was shifted back towards the latter – at least in western Europe. Yet each, perhaps fitfully, links the nineteenth century with the twentieth and shapes the world in which we live.

Ascendancy and decline; confidence and doubt

Nevertheless, necessary though it may be to recognize how the nineteenth century forms the pre-history of the twentieth, in looking back over the themes studied in this course you should not forget how different the nineteenth century was from the twentieth. We should be careful not to make the unfamiliar artificially familiar. A major difference between the Europe of the nineteenth century and the Europe of the twentieth is capture in the title of the set book, *The Ascendancy of Europe*. The nineteenth century was the century of Europe's ascendancy; the twentieth century has been the century of Europe's relative decline – a decline which was in part inevitable. The rest of the world has caught up with and in many respects overtaken the continent which was:

1   the first to industrialize and use its economic and military supremacy to establish empires which covered the globe, but which squandered so much of the material and spiritual achievement of the nineteenth century in the enormous bloodletting of the twentieth;

2   the first to develop the modern bureaucratic state and state-organized systems of social welfare – but which saw states develop into monstrous machines capable of carrying out crimes against humanity of proportions previously unimaginable;

3   the first to form modern nation-states on the basis of nationalist sentiment and nationalist politics, which provided both a model for the rest of the world and cause of debilitating conflict.

The contrast between the European ascendancy of the nineteenth century and the relative decline of the twentieth can be seen clearly in the economic sphere. Until the First World War, the centre of the world economic and financial system was London; during the First World War, with the suspension of the gold convertibility of sterling and growing demands upon the Exchequer made by the needs of the war and the growing financial dependence of Britain upon the United States, this changed, so that after the conflict the centre of the world financial system was New York. The centre of the world economy shifted from the Old World to the New. A similar shift may be observed in diplomatic sphere, where the importance of the old European powers (Britain, France, Germany) was eclipsed during the twentieth century by that of the United States and the Soviet Union. In his treatise on *The Rise and Fall of the Great Powers*, which climbed up the best-seller lists on the eve of the collapse of the USSR, Paul Kennedy introduced his chapter on 'the coming of a bipolar world' with the observation:

> In the winter of 1884–1885, the Great Powers of the world, joined by a few smaller states, met in Berlin in an attempt to reach an agreement over trade, navigation, and boundaries in West Africa and the Congo and the principles of effective occupation more generally. In so many ways, the Berlin West Africa Conference can be seen, symbolically, as the zenith of Old Europe's period of predominance in global affairs. ... The centre of affairs was ... the triangular relationship

between London, Paris, and Berlin, with Bismarck in the all-import-ant middle position. The fate of the planet still appeared to rest where it had seemed to rest for the preceding century or more: in the chancelleries of Europe. To be sure if the conference had been decid-ing the future of the Ottoman Empire instead of the Congo Basin, the countries such as Austria-Hungary and Russia would have played a larger role. But that still would not gainsay what was reckoned at the time to be an incontrovertible truth: that Europe was the centre of the world. ...

Within another three decades – a short time indeed in the course of the Great Power system – that same continent of Europe would be tearing itself apart and several of its members would be close to collapse. Three decades further, and the end would be com-plete, much of the continent would be economically devastated parts of it would be in ruins, and its very future would be in the hands of decision-makers in Washington and Moscow. (Kennedy, 1987, pp. 194–5)

What Max Weber had predicted during the First World War, namely that Germany's continuing struggle effectively was paving the way for the supremacy of America and Russia, seemed largely to have come true.

The contrast between the history of nineteenth-century Europe and that of twentieth-century Europe could hardly be sharper. Europe's ascendancy has been halted and reversed; Europe no longer is 'the centre of the world'. Yet the Europe of the twentieth century is the child of the Europe of the nineteenth; the Europe whose history you have studied in A221 is the parent of the Europe in which you have lived. The 'ascendancy', of Europe created the preconditions for its relative decline, and we cannot understand our Europe without understanding its relation-ship to the Europe which preceded it.

Exercise   If you had to put into a single phrase, or single word, what you think the history of Europe in the nineteenth century was about, what would you say it was? (Another way of putting it is: What single theme do you think unites the various subjects which you have studied in this course?.) This is hardly an easy question, but after working your way through the course materials and Anderson's *The Ascendancy of Europe*, you ought to have some ideas of how to answer.

Discussion   You may have come up with a different answer, but I would respond to such a question with the word 'progress'. In all the main themes of this course – state, economy, nation – we are talking about growth, improve-ment, expansion, or (to use Anderson's apposite term) 'ascendancy'. The nineteenth century was the century in which the European state grew (though obviously at different rates in different countries), became more bureaucratic (in the positive, descriptive, ideal-typical sense of the term), reached out to affect the lives of more Europeans. The nineteenth century was the era of classic industrialization and urbanization in Europe: the economic and social history of nineteenth-century Europe is shown against the backdrop of vast economic expansion, the growth and progress of great cities and great industries. The nineteenth century also was, as we have seen, the century in which European nationalism took root and spread, so

TMA4

that one could speak of the growth of national consciousness. It was a century in which education and literacy spread enormously, enormously extending the horizons of millions of Europeans. And, of course, it was the century during which Europeans established a hegemony over much of the globe. So, in each of these spheres, one might speak of 'progress' or (to employ the somewhat less value-laden term of Anderson) 'ascendancy'; certainly during the nineteenth century many Europeans could feel some satisfaction at the material progress they witnessed and some confidence that it would continue.

Nevertheless (as you will remember if you have read Anderson through to the end!), this positive picture of progress was beginning to disintegrate as the nineteenth century drew to a close. The certainties of the nineteenth century were becoming subjected to increasing challenge, a process which developed with such terrible manifestations in the twentieth (our) century, and this is the theme with which I would like to conclude the course.

Exercise   Please turn again to Anderson, and read (re-read?) the final section ('The Exploration of Consciousness and the Growth of Self-Doubt') of Chapter 7 (pp.358–69). As outlined in its title, this section essentially has two themes: changing political consciousness and cultural manifestations of doubt. Let us begin with the political consciousness and political ideologies outlined by Anderson. Anderson focuses on the development of two broad strands of political thought and action: on the one hand, radical political ideologies – such as syndicalism. Marxian socialism, anarchism – largely (but not exclusively) supported by poorer, working people; on the other, liberalism. I would like to pose three questions about the two broad strands of political 'consciousness'.

1   What have these two strands in common (how do they approach the issue of 'progress')?   socialism <> liberalism

2   What differentiates them?

3   What, according to Anderson, constituted the most fundamental challenge to optimistic ideologies of progress such as liberalism at the end of the nineteenth century?

Specimen Answers and   1   They are both ideologies of 'progress', and they both presuppose that
Discussion   what motivates human beings, whether in the political, economic or social sphere, is essentially rational. The political force and attractions of both liberalism and socialism were drawn (in part) from a conviction that one could speak confidently of historical development and that this development would be a positive, progressive one. In the case of liberalism, this conviction was based on 'transcendental truths' and 'the absolute value of the individual' (Anderson, p.362). In the case of Marxian ('scientific') socialism, this conviction was based on a materialist conception of history moving inexorably in a particular direction. Behind the discontent which fuelled support for socialist (as well as mutualist, syndicalist or even anarchist) ideologies in late nineteenth-century Europe there lay a conviction that inevitable historical development and/or collective action would lead to improvement.

RISORGIMENTO

2   One could speak here of the fundamental difference between (liberal) ideologies whereby the individual stands at the centre and (socialist) ideologies which view the world and politics within a collective framework. Of course, many nineteenth-century liberals may have felt uneasy about, or been concerned to exclude from the political process, individuals who for various reasons (such as lack of education) they felt could not be trusted to exercise rational judgement; and of course many proponents of collectivist ideologies tended to ignore the interests of groups as groups (such as women) which seem of obvious importance to us today. But the difference is a clear one. However, I would choose to highlight something else: on the one hand, the loss of confidence (underlined by Anderson) which political liberalism suffered in the late nineteenth century and, on the other, the growing confidence particularly of Marxists and non-Marxist socialists (or syndicalists or anarchists) that their time was coming. The two were, of course, related. The decline of liberalism has much to do with the rise of democratic pressures, and the challenge of representing the poorer and labouring classes in the political system. This challenge was posed most powerfully by socialist movements.

3   The answer to this question is fairly clear. Towards the bottom of p.364 Anderson identifies what he describes as the 'most insidious adversary' of nineteenth-century liberal thought: 'new views of the nature of man, both as an individual and as a part of society, which were being put forward by a number of profoundly original thinkers ... [who were] preoccupied with the irrational and non-rational aspects of human psychology'. The optimistic beliefs in progress which had gained so much ground in the nineteenth century were based upon the assumption that people behave rationally. This assumption was challenged, as Anderson notes, by thinkers with such widely diverse viewpoints as Georges Sorel and Sigmund Freud, who did not regard human behaviour as necessarily rational. Anderson also sees (p.366) 'the growing disintegration of old certainties of belief – in the essential rationality of man [!], in the reality of progress – ... the end of the century in a growing rejection of fixed standards' in European cultural life.

In the second portion of Chapter 7, where Anderson focuses on intellectual and artistic trends, such as the 'progressive abandonment of the idea of fixed tonality in music' and the 'reaction against realism' in the visual arts, he develops the interesting contrast between the still widespread faith in progress held by 'the ordinary man' and cultural expressions of uncertainty, confusion and self-doubt. Whereas 'the ordinary man' could point to improvement in health, prosperity and comfort (at least in many places in western Europe) and maintain a faith in scientific progress and social evolution, Europe's intellectual avant-garde were entertaining ideas 'distrustful of, even destructive of, such hopes and certainties' (pp.368–9). That the uncertainties of the intellectuals, rather than the faith of the masses, were to receive their confirmation after 1914 provides Anderson

with justification for contrasting two end points for the nineteenth century:
'Politically the nineteenth century ended in 1914. In the world of ideas and
the arts the beginning of the end for nineteenth-century Europe had come
two decades earlier' (p.368). The apparent certainties and belief in progress and 'ascendancy' which remained common currency in the political
sphere (even, perhaps especially, among Marxist opponents of the political
systems and structures of the day), already were under significant attack
on the ideas front. The doubt and uncertainties which were expressed with
greatest force and clarity in the cultural sphere may be seen to have had
their terrible confirmation when, after August 1914, Europe plunged head-
long into the century of world wars, dictatorship and genocide. With the
advent of the twentieth century, it became increasingly difficult to hold
onto that belief which had been so widespread in the nineteenth, the belief
in 'the essential rationality of man'.

An end to progress?

It is probably impossible to choose *the* observation or *the* development or
juxtaposition which can neatly sum up the relationship of Europe in the
nineteenth century to Europe in the twentieth. My own predilection is to
view the history of the twentieth century as in large measure the destruction of the apparent certainties and beliefs in progress which had developed so confidently in the nineteenth. This may be a consequence of
overemphasizing the catastrophes of Europe's twentieth century and
underestimating the dark side of the nineteenth; after all, one should not
forget that nineteenth-century Europeans witnessed the first modern economic crises (i.e. depressions which were not essentially a consequence of
the weather), great-power rivalry, savage repression (as in post-1848
Europe, in the aftermath of the Paris Commune of 1871 or in Tsarist Russia) and the grinding poverty of tens of millions of people. Nevertheless, it
is difficult to ignore the fact that Europe's nineteenth century, a century of
relative peace, prosperity, optimism and ascendancy, was followed on
European soil by the greatest slaughter and the most savage economic
depressions the world has known; whatever the word one might choose
with which to describe the history of twentieth-century Europe,
'ascendancy' is not it.

　　This stress on doubt and uncertainty is the reason why the subtitle of
this concluding essay ends with a question mark: 'The Making of Modern
Europe?' As we have seen, one could view the history of nineteenth-century Europe as the realization of visions of progress, as a history of ascendancy which left Europe in a dominant position in the world and Europeans
among the most prosperous people on the globe. But the doubts expressed
as Europe's nineteenth century closed, and the horrors which followed,
make me think that an attempt to draw up a balance sheet on the history
of nineteenth-century Europe needs to include an expression of the doubt
and ambivalence with which the legacy of the nineteenth century has been
viewed.

This is not to claim that explanations of all the disasters of the twentieth century lie in tracing things back through time to the nineteenth. Three interrelated objections to such a one-sided approach might be put forward. First, to judge the nineteenth century solely in terms of the negative aspects of the twentieth is to fail to appreciate the nineteenth century on its own terms, or to assume that the cultural pessimism which became increasingly prevalent towards the end of the nineteenth century was representative of the whole of the century for the whole of Europe. Second, viewing the relatively stable nineteenth century solely as the prehistory of the 'age of extremes' in the twentieth may cause us to lose sight of the magnitude of the (positive) transformations which did take place in the nineteenth century. One such is the greatest human migration which the world had ever known – of tens of millions of Europeans to North and South America and Australasia – during the long nineteenth century. And third, such an approach runs the danger of losing sight of how different Europe's nineteenth century was from the twentieth – for example, of the degree to which the First World War was a watershed. Nevertheless, one inescapable element of 'history', as presented and interpreted by historians, is chronology, 'what comes next?'. The twentieth century did follow the nineteenth; the ways in which Europeans viewed their world in the twentieth century was, in large measure, inherited from the nineteenth century, and the history of the twentieth century was shaped by the legacy of the nineteenth.

There can be few more poignant reminders of how the intellectual legacy of nineteenth-century Europe – the values of European Enlightenment culture – collided with the realities of the twentieth century than Isaac Deutscher's description of his father Jacob. I find it a particularly thought-provoking comment on the cultures and histories of nineteenth- and twentieth-century Europe, and it strikes me therefore as perhaps a fitting way to close this course. Deutscher, a Polish Jew who joined the Polish Communist Party after the First World War, subsequently emigrated to Britain and became famous as the biographer of Trotsky, said in a television interview a month before he died in 1967:

> My father was an orthodox Jew, in love with German culture, philosophy, and poetry. ... He was always wanting to read German literature and German periodicals with me. He had himself, in his youth, published essays in the *Neue Freie Presse*, the best-known Viennese newspaper; had been correspondent of the Warsaw *Hazefra*, the first daily to appear in the Hebrew language; and had also written a little book in Hebrew about Spinoza, with the Latin title *Amor Dei Intellectualis*. Spinoza was one of his heroes; Heine the other. My father also had great respect for Lassalle, but the highest intellectual ideal for him, apart from Hebrew writers was, of course, Goethe. I did not share my father's partiality for German poetry. I was a Polish patriot. Mickiewicz and Slowacki were incomparably dearer and closer to me. For this reason I never learned the German language thoroughly either. My father often used to say to me: 'Yes, you want to write all your fine poetry only in Polish. I know you will be a great writer one day' – for my father had quite an exaggerated idea of my literary talent, and wanted me to exercise it in a 'world language'. 'German', he would say, 'is *the* world language. Why should you bury all your talent in a provincial language? You have only to go beyond Auschwitz ...' – Auschwitz was just near us, on the frontier –

'you have only to go beyond Auschwitz, and practically nobody will understand you any more, you and your fine Polish language. You really must learn German.' That was his ever-recurring refrain: 'You have only to go beyond Auschwitz and you will be totally lost, my son!' Impatient as I was, I often interrupted him: 'I already know what you are going to say, father – You have only to go beyond Auschwitz, and you will be lost.'

The tragic truth is that my father never went beyond Auschwitz. During the Second World War he disappeared into Auschwitz. (Deutscher, 1968, pp. 18–20)

References

Breuilly, J. (1992), *Labour and Liberalism in Nineteenth-Century Europe. Essays in Comparative History*, Manchester University Press, Manchester.

Deutscher, I. (1968), *The Non-Jewish Jew and other Essays*, Oxford University Press, London.

Kennedy, P. (1987), *The Rise and Fall of the Great Powers. Economic Change and Military Conflict from 1500 to 2000*, Random House, New York.

Mason, T. (1993), *Social Policy in the Third Reich. The Working Class and the 'National Community'*, Berg, Providence and Oxford.

Index

Dea KELLY

40 Fordwich Close

Allington
Maidstone
Kent ME16 0NU

DaisyK 1962 @ aol.com